Heghlegh Then
and
Heeley Now

Work, Play and People

As recalled and researched by members of the Heeley History Workshop

Opened in 1826, the Wesleyan Chapel at the corner of Gleadless Road/Hartley Street. In 1926, 5,000 people attended an open air Centenary Service here, from all the Churches in Heeley.

Pickards Publishing 2000

Acknowledgements

Thanks to all the members of the Heeley History Workshop, past and present; to Sheffield Local Studies Library and all the staff there; to Sheffield Archives and the staff there too; to the Sheffield Star for the use of photos and everyone else who lent us pictures. (A complete listing is at the back of the book).

Thanks to the Millennium Awards for All for giving us the money to make this book happen and thanks to the Heeley Development Trust, especially Tess Bruckner, without whom we wouldn't have even tried to get the Millennium Award grant.

Thanks to our families and friends for being patient with us when we couldn't talk about anything other than Heeley or when we stayed up all night writing and typing.

Thanks to all the people out there who ordered copies of this book when it was only a bit of wishful thinking and gave us the determination to carry on.

Printed by
Pickards Colour Publishing
Unit 11 Riverside Park
Sheaf Gardens
Sheffield S2 4BB
Telephone: 0114 275 7222/444

Heghlegh Then and Heeley Now
Contents

'What is the use of a book', thought Alice, 'without pictures or conversation?'
'Alice's Adventures in Wonderland' (1865).
Lewis Carroll, 1832 ~ 1898.

'There is a history
in all men's lives ···'
'Henry iv,' Part II. (1597).
William Shakespeare 1564 ~ 1616.

'There is no history of mankind, there are only many histories of all kinds of aspects of human life.'
'The Open Society and its Enemies.' (1945).
Sir Karl Popper, 1902 ~ 1994

Introduction

Heeley gets its name from Heah Leah, which means a high woodland clearing. Various spellings of the name have been discovered in ancient charters including Heghlegh and Heylaye. The hamlet was divided into Upper and Nether Heeley in the earliest directories, later the Nether became Lower and Middle Heeley was added halfway up the hill.

The Meers Brook flowing between the gardens in 1950 looking towards the end of Northcote Avenue

The Meers Brook, which forms the southern boundary of Heeley parish, was also the boundary between Yorkshire and Derbyshire until recently. Previously the brook had been the important marker between the ancient kingdoms of Northumbria and Mercia and between the archbishoprics of York and Lichfield.

"I lived in Albert Road, at the end of a long row of houses. At one end there was Boulby's corner shop —
then twelve houses. I lived at the opposite end to the shop and we had a nice long garden leading down to the brook which flowed through what we called the Bottom. Seeing that nearly every house had 5 or 6 children we were never short of playmates and spent countless hours messing about on the river in-spite of endless warnings about getting our shoes wet and weird tales about Mary Blood who would one day kidnap us. She was supposed to live in the tunnel which opened in our yard and went through to Brooklyn Road.

A great event was when a cow got stuck in the tunnel. I think it was going to the slaughter house which was in Valley Road, near the mission Church, before that was bombed in the war. A crowd of us children were watching the attempts to drive the animal through with much pushing and prodding by some men. At last out it rushed and we scattered all over knocking one another over in our haste.

We used to walk down the river from Kent Road, along the backs of houses in Albert Road. In summer it was evil-smelling and sluggish, but in winter it could get really deep and swollen bringing all sorts of rubbish with it, hen huts, dead cats and once a dog. I expect they had been dumped by their owners.

The Meers Brook just before it goes under Brooklyn Road. 1961.

I think it was culverted around 1962 and we were sad, in a way, to see it go. It held so many memories of long days in the holidays playing there. It was the nearest most of us ever got to the seaside. My brothers pulled a big tree out and placed it across the brook and we all imagined it was a liner, sailing to America. I'm sure we had much more fun then with simple things, that cost nothing more than a little imagination and make-believe. This picture was taken by my sister showing the wall which separated the river from Brooklyn Road."
Mrs A Bell (age 93 in 2000)

When the parish of Heeley was first established in 1846 as a daughter parish of St Mary's Bramall Lane, it extended from the Derbyshire border by the Meers Brook and the River Sheaf to Harmer Lane, near Pond Street, up Bungay Street and Talbot Street to Intake (now City) Road. The parish included Norfolk Park, Lower, Middle and Upper Heeley, Newfield Green and the farms and big houses from the Park up to the top of the present Arbourthorne estate. By 1953 the boundaries ran along London Road to Heeley Bridge and the Meers Brook, up across the western edge of Arbourthorne, through the middle of Norfolk Park Estate to the junction of Farm Road and Granville Road and then back along Queen's Road to London Road. Parts of the original Heeley parish are now in Park, Abbeydale, St Aidan's and St Leonard's districts.

The White's Trade Directory of 1879 describes the situation of Heeley in those days.
"Heeley (originally High Ley) is a detached member of Nether Hallam, containing 3860 inhabitants, living on 305 acres; it is 2 to 3 miles distant from the rest of the township; but its ecclesiastical parish, formed in 1846, and having a population of 7197, living in 1510 houses on 1214 acres includes part of Sheffield Park. Until the sale of Mr Shore's estates, about 28 years ago, the village of Heeley had experienced but little improvement during the past century; but the picturesque dale between it and the Meersbrook rivulet is now divided into freehold garden allotments under the name of the Shirebrook Estate; and on the other sides of Lower, Middle and Upper Heeley several large fields have been divided into building and garden plots. Good roads have been made, and many house and cottages have been erected on these freehold estates during the last 20 years. The Chesterfield and Sheffield new diversion of the trunk line of the Midland Railway has a passenger station as well as a large mineral depot here."

"Heeley must have been a lovely picturesque area in the early 1800s before the arrival of the railway and all the different industries. I remember my Dad telling me he remembered his mother, nee Ruth Woodcock, who as a child had lived on Sheaf Bank, talking about the trout in the River Sheaf and being able to see the ducks on the pond (Heeley Tilt) from their house. She told Dad they had a boat tied up at the bottom of their garden. Also grandma remembered standing in their garden waving to the passengers on the first train through Heeley around 1870." *Joyce Jenkinson (nee Boot)*

Albert Richards, who also lived on Sheaf Bank, and his playmates used to build rafts that they could float on the Sheaf when it was in flood. This would have been during the 1940s.

Ruth (nee Woodcock) and Albert Boot, Joyce Jenkinsons's Grandparents, about 1920

Heeley Toll Bar marked the crossing into Derbyshire on the turnpike road and was the scene of a daring robbery in 1839. A traveller was attacked by five rogues, who took his hat, umbrella and money.

Heeley Toll Bar: The Meers Brook flows under the road here and joins the River Sheaf to the right of the sketch, behind the houses. The old gas lamp would have needed a lamplighter to come around with his pole to light it.
Sheffield Local Studies Library

"As a child I wondered why Heeley was often referred to as Heeley Duff'em. When I eventually plucked up courage to ask what 'Duff'em' meant I was shocked to learn that it meant, in the words of my informant, anxious to air his knowledge of local affairs, "Refusing to pay money 'what you owed", dodging debts in other words.

My parents never owed a penny and as neighbours seemed to be honest enough, after all they always paid you back in kind if they borrowed a bag of sugar, a loaf or any other item. I thought it grossly unfair to give such a nickname to what I considered to be one of Sheffield's more select suburbs. Why not Ecclesall Duff'em, Attercliffe Duff'em or dare I say it Fulwood or Ranmoor Duff'em. Was it because their residents were more honest?

Various suggestions have been offered to explain the reason for the unenviable name of Heeley Duff'em. It didn't sound right – Heeley on the Sheaf would have been acceptable but Heeley Duff'em – never!

Apparently as soon as the debt collector or bailiff appeared on the scene the message would be passed along a row of terraced houses that he was on his way. A tap on the neighbour's kitchen wall would be passed on to the end of the row. When the unfortunate bailiff or debt collector knocked on his

The Footbridge over the Meers Brook at the lowest point of Kent Road 1930s looking towards Rushdale Avenue. This gas lamp would light up on a time switch and it contained a warning to motorists showing 'No Through Road'.
Sheffield Local Studies Library.

victim's door there would be no answer. I was told that one silly woman, in her excitement to give the impression that nobody was at home, foolishly shouted out, "We're not in".

Perhaps here is the truth at last:

The Meersbrook divided Yorkshire and Derbyshire which meant that Heeley was a border district. The spot close to Heeley Toll Bar was the nearest to Derbyshire. Sheffield County Court bailiffs had no authority to serve summons for debt on people in Derbyshire, so it was easy for defaulters to slip across the border before the bailiff could catch them. Naturally Heeley was a good place to live, as Derbyshire people could cross into Yorkshire to give the slip to the Derbyshire bailiffs and Yorkshire folk could slip over into Derbyshire.

However all good things come to an end. The passing of a County Court jurisdiction into Derbyshire as far as Norton and Greenhill meant that Heeley lost its popularity as a safe haven for both Yorkshire and Derbyshire debt dodgers. Sadly or happily, whichever way you look at it, Heeley is still called Heeley Duff'em by those in the know and it is with a certain amount of pride that they'll tell a stranger the 'true' story." **Alun Montgomery**

The area was originally an agricultural settlement with cottage industries in cutlery and file making. Along the valley of the River Sheaf, which forms the western boundary of Heeley and even on the Meers Brook in the old Rush Dale, were several ponds and wheels.

"Heeley Wheel is marked on some surveys as "Heeley Side Old Corn Mill" but its life as a grinding wheel was much longer than as a corn mill so the olden name is retained. There is considerable evidence to prove that there were several grinding wheels in this vicinity as far back as the year 1550. A rent book of the Manor of Hallamshire for 1604 includes "John Pearson. Heylie Wheel. £3.0.0 per annum.", and in Harrison's Survey of 1637 it is recorded that Widow Pearson paid Five Pounds per annum for "Heeley Wheel containing three cutlers wheeles in two houses at Heeley Bridge". In 1717 a lease granted to John Lee in 1716 by Thomas, Duke of Norfolk for 21 years for £8.12.6 a year, of the Cutler Wheel, called Heeley Wheel consisting of two ends and two troughs with weirs etc., was assigned by John Lee, barber chirurgien to Joshua Rose of Heeley, cutler; Samuel Smith of Heeley, file cutter, to occupy half and pay half the rent. It is also marked as a cutler's wheel on a survey of 1740, and is labelled as Mr Taylor's Wheel on a plan dated 1770. It is called a "disused grinding wheel" in 1775, but in 1794 a Mr Wigfall was said to be working eight "trows" here employing ten men, and in 1801 Wigfull Peters ran eight "trows". So far as it is known John Kinder was the last to work it as a grinding wheel up to about 1850. After this it appears to have been changed into a corn mill and William Bagshaw and George Birkinshaw are recorded as millers at "Lower Heeley" in 1854. These premises were taken over with Heeley Mill in 1864 by Mr Sidney Parker, the miller, but Heeley Wheel disappeared with the advent of the Midland Railway and now lies buried under Heeley Station." **Leslie Molyneux**

AW Booker wrote about Heeley Hall, an ancient 17th century building that once stood behind Ye Olde Shakespeare Inn on Well Road.

"Whilst Cavalier and Roundhead were striving for mastery in the Civil War … Heeley Hall was being built and was completed in 1643. The name of the builders we do not know but as we are told, a family of the name of Gill and their descendants lived in it for nearly two centuries, probably the founder would be a relative of Captain Gill, the governor of Sheffield Castle after its surrender to the Parliamentary forces in 1644 and whose family resided at Norton. This gentleman evidently had an idea of strength and beauty of situation for the walls of the Hall, what was left of them, were nearly two feet in thickness and as for the situation the Hall was built on rising ground near what is now the Shakespeare Inn. The inmates would have glorious aspect of Hill and Dale, Woodland and Moorland; to the south over Springwood, part of which reached down to the Meers Brook, to the Moors of Totley and the hills of the Peak, or over the belt of Oaks which later became Oak Street across the Abbey Dale to the heights beyond. This last reference in relation to these trees was in 1854 when some of their stumps were used as points of vantage to watch the soldiers march past on their way to the Crimean War. However the last Tenants who resided at Heeley Hall were two brothers, who in the latter half of the century made part of the Hall into Cutlers' Workshops. The greater part of the Hall was demolished many years ago, and when seen by the writer all that remained was a three story building called the Chapel,

altered later to a dwelling house , with oblong windows of the period, and some outbuildings and stables which one may say in passing Mr Wilson, who drove what was popularly known as "The Heeley Mail", stabled his donkeys. As for the inside of the main building nothing but bare walls and oak beams were to be seen, with the exception of the front room where remains of Mythological and Scroll plaster mouldings were still to be seen, one over the fireplace being that of a figure, part woman, part dragon, playing a harp. To look around the grinning faces and grotesque figures, which bordered the ceiling, one was struck by the peculiar idea of ornament possessed by the inmates."

Mrs Birkinshaw (aged 85 in 1987) recalled playing amongst the rubble and swinging on the remaining beams of the old hall when as a young child her parents lived at the Shakespeare around 1918. Her father, who had two or three horses, used to house them in the derelict stables of the old hall. There are descriptions too of underground passages from the Hall to Sheffield Manor. The only remaining sign of the long occupation of Heeley is the cruck barn on Wilson Place, for much of the 20th century a working foundry. A farmhouse, home of the Boot family, ancestors of Henry Boot the builders, stood across the road from the pub at the top of Oak Street. After the Oak Street Chapel was built in 1871 one long low building was converted into two classrooms and survived until the 1970s as a community room. Above the doorway was a lintel carved with the inscription 'I.S. 1658'.

An agricultural community needed water and the wells and springs in Heeley are recalled in the names Well Road, Well Head Road and maybe Springwood Road.

"There are lots of wells – both discovered and undiscovered - in Heeley. From the top of Gleadless right down to the Sheaf on Heeley Bottom in various places the ground seems to be like an inverted colander with water springing up in unlikely places. Behind the Cuckoo(Prospect View pub) on Gleadless Road was a pond where boys used to catch newts and the ground was swampy. There was a pond near Meersbrook Park and there is still a small pond in Far Lees near Newfield School. The latter was a constructed 'mere' to provide water for Cockshutt Farm, demolished to make way for Newfield School. In the 1920s there were rainbow and brown trout in the brook in Cat Lane near Rose Cottage. There are memories of boys catching trout and cooking them in the woods and of damming up the rivers to make small reservoirs of water for bathing in school holidays."
HHW

Water Pump on Artisan View

Water for washing, drinking and cooking would have to be fetched from pumps in the yards and streets.

"My grandmother lived in a big yard at the top of Heeley Green before you came to the centre of the many shops which abounded in Heeley. There was a big wall at the back of Moody's then on to Cross Myrtle Road where South's (previously Crowther's) shop was on the corner. It finished there and then it started to go back up Myrtle Road. The wall came right round the houses at the back of my grandmother's house up to Myrtle Road. In this yard there were about ten houses. In Heeley Green there were four, two above and two below the entrance, no gate but a big entrance. There was another big yard above with a pump in it. There were about five houses in the yard above. This goes to Myrtle Road and there was an opening. I can remember the pump, but I can't remember it being used. I suppose they had to fetch water from the pump to use in the kitchen."
Mr Eddie Chapman aged 98 in 2000.

Eddie Chapman with his grandparents, Thomas and Florence Ibberson around 1910

In the late nineteenth and early twentieth centuries Heeley would have been quite self-sufficient for shops, school, church and all the other necessities of life.

Mrs Norah Bramhill's grandparents Mr and Mrs Albert Henry Denton lived at a small shop at 11 Alexandra Road. She relates the stories told her by her mother, born in 1881, the eldest of six children.

"As a small girl she used to stand outside the shop on Saturdays selling oranges from the box at a halfpenny each to men and boys coming to the Sheffield Wednesday matches at Olive Grove. This was quite a luxury in those days. She was sent when money was permitting to a 'Ladies School' at the sum of one penny per week. This was before the days of free education. This school was held in the building at the corner of Gleadless Road and Hartley Street which was a Methodist Chapel and I can still read the remains of the name on the stone in the upper part of this building. I think the day school was only for girls, but I am not sure. It was a private school run by two ladies – hence its name – a Ladies School. They taught reading, writing, arithmetic and spelling but little else. Each afternoon they had sewing, needlework, crocheting and knitting. These skills however lasted her all her life, and she had clever fingers.

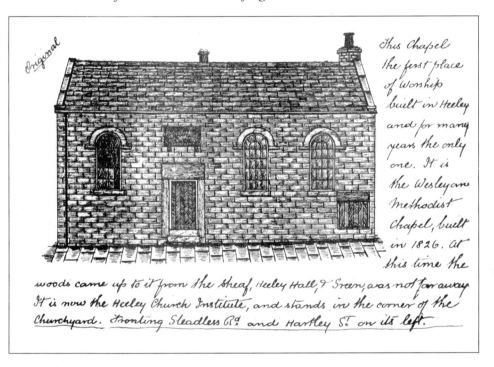

Original

This Chapel the first place of worship built in Heeley and for many years the only one. It is the Wesleyan Methodist Chapel, built in 1826. At this time the woods came up to it from the Sheaf, Heeley Hall, & Green, was not far away It is now the Heeley Church Institute, and stands in the corner of the Churchyard. Fronting Gleadless Rd and Hartley St on its left.

Heeley Chapel from Henry Tatton's Notebook - drawn about 1930.
Sheffield Local Studies Library.

Myrtle Road was considered very 'upper class' at that time and Grandma took in a bit of laundry. She used to wash and starch stiff, round collars for the gentlemen. Mother had the job of dollying half a tub at once and as a child I used to play with a round iron (not a flat iron) which was the iron she or Grandma had used for the job of ironing them.

Of course she had to leave school and go out to work at an early age and she was employed in Dixon's Silver Warehouse, Cornish Place, Shalesmoor. The hours were 8am to 6pm and she had to walk there and back. This meant getting up at 6.30am. Grandma often mistook the time by Grandpa's watch and Mother was then called at 5.30am. This did not matter as she then had time to knead up a stone (14lbs) of bread ready for Grandma to bake for the shop.

This leads me to a winter about this time when she got to Havelock Bridge and the workmen who were clearing the snow lifted her over. It must have been a very hard winter because most of the outside water pipes froze. [Most houses had a pump.] Grandma had done so much baking that hers lasted longer than most of those around. Hers was allowed to run night and day to keep it flowing and people came and helped themselves to water from the tap [on the outside wall of the kitchen or living room]. Eventually it did freeze up and water had to be carried from a standpipe in the yard of the Earl of Arundel." **Norah Bramhill.**

Articles in our booklets such as the one above have prompted ex-Heeleyites to write to us with their own stories of Heeley.

"My father and mother were born and married in Heeley and although I was born in Liverpool (my father moved us there to obtain work in the 1929 slump) I came back to Sheffield with the family in 1932 when I was nine months old and lived in Kent Road from the age of 2 to 15 years old. I remember these years very well and have lots of happy memories.

My father was unemployed and as we were all members of the church my father used to go and garden at the vicarage for Mr and Mrs Kendall. Mrs Kendall was a doctor and they had two children Mary and Nigel. I used to go with Dad sometimes and Mary and I used to play together in the garden. We used to go into the kitchen at the vicarage for milk and as they had a maid I thought they were very posh! …

Just below our house in Kent Road - we lived at number 46 and my grandma lived at number 54 – was a little general grocery store owned by Mr and Mrs Kelly, then came Cambridge Street and below that a chip shop run by Mr and Mrs Hughes. At Easter time Mr Hughes always had small chocolate Easter eggs in the shop for the children who fetched the chips and fish. Further along was Mrs Bentley's shop where she sold the teacakes and bread she baked herself. Powder cakes were her speciality, they were delicious…

Mum still lived at home after she married as Dad was in the Army in France. One night she went to visit a friend at Pitsmoor and because she got home at 10pm my Grandma burnt the hat she was wearing and told her she would write to Dad and tell him that Mum was a loose woman!"
Thelma Elliot nee Styring.

In the chapters ahead we will be focusing on some of the features of Heeley from the last few centuries remembered or researched by our members. We will investigate the worlds of work, leisure, school and play, seen through the eyes of those who lived here in time now past. Treat this book as an introduction to Heeley but please do not expect an all-encompassing history, as we are sure that there are many stories still out there yet to be told.

Looking down Kent Road towards Rushdale over the Meers Brook now covered over.

Rural to Industrial

The name given to Heeley in Middle English suggests an agricultural district in a hilly area, the term 'heah' or 'hegh' means high and 'leah' or 'legh' means a ley or meadow in a wooded clearing. It is known that 2000 years ago most of this countryside was wooded. At the time of the first millennium AD only limited areas of woodland had been cleared for house and boat building, furniture making and fuel, for use in crop growing or animal grazing. Studies of woodlands that exist in Heeley now in 2000 AD show that some are ancient woodlands and have been persistent in those sites for centuries. The evidence

Heeley Common Cottages, now demolished. Sheffield Local Studies Library

provided by the species and distribution of the trees and the occurrence and spread of the undergrowth flora (such as Dog's Mercury, Wood Anemones, Wood Sorrel and Bluebells) indicates that the Cat Lane and Lees Hall woods and Rollestone wood (the Rolling) existed a very long time ago.

In times past the common people would have grazing rights in the woodland areas. They would have been able to allow such animals as pigs to feed on the acorns and beech mast on the woodland floor in the autumn and would have harvested nuts for winter fodder. At the same time there was probably some early industry in woodland clearings. Evidence of coal pits for early open cast mining have been found. There is pictorial evidence of water wheels on the rivers forming our boundaries, both the Sheaf and the Meers Brook provided enough water power for mills in which trows for knife grinding and scythe sharpening were operated. Flour milling was carried out at Blythe's mill on the Meers Brook.

The steps which used to lead to the cottages pictured above, still in existence in 2000

An engraving of Heeley Tilt Mill Dam from 1791.

"Heeley Mill 'Hiley Milne on the Broad Water called Sheve' is mentioned in many old deeds and charters. It was in being before 1600 and an indenture of 1608 specifies that John Parker of Lees Hall was the owner by inheritance of the 'Watercorne Mill at Hyley'. No records have been found covering the next 120 years but in 1730 'John Hatfield of Laughton le Morthing' leased to George Hobson of Heeley 'a water grist mill called Heeley Mill with three pairs of stones and toll custome and benefit of grinding corne and graine' for sixteen years at an annual rent of fifteen pounds. George Hobson, miller, is given as party to various leases up to 1766, so it is assumed that the family retained the mill for many years. John Brailsforth or Brailsford was the miller here in 1806 and up to about 1830 and the four-storied mill which stood within the huddle of the surrounding buildings was erected for the Brailsfords about 1834. It contained six pairs of millstones driven by two water wheels. In the directories of 1841 and 1845 the tenants are given as Mary and John Brailsford, but they apparently gave up the mill before 1854. After that the records are confused but it is believed that a miller by the name of Greasy or Greaser occupied the premises for a time and in 1864 the mill was taken over by Mr Sidney Parker who was followed by his son Mr A J Parker, by whom it was run up to 1920 or thereabouts with the aid of a gas engine." **Leslie Molyneux**

Large trees felled for houses and barn building created spaces that could be used for crop growing and animal grazing. A large farmhouse, opposite the front of the present Shakespeare Inn and Heeley Hall, which was just behind the Inn, were probably built in the seventeenth century. Cruck barns, with giant oak beams and supports used in their construction, would have stood nearby. The farmhouse, occupied by the Boot family for generations, was pulled down and Oak Street Chapel was built on its site in 1871, while one of its barns was retained for use as a lecture hall and Sunday School rooms for the Chapel.

The old Heeley Hall was eventually used by the Wheatcroft family for file cutting and was in ruins by the early years of the twentieth century. Part of its cruck barn is still in existence, for many years it was

known as Ernest Wright's Foundry and its cruck beam construction was obvious when you looked inside.

Inside Wright's Foundry around 1960s.
Sheffield Local Studies Library

By the early eighteenth century parts of Heeley were cleared of woodland and used for strip farming or crofting. The rising land used for strip farming (now occupied by Myrtle, Alexandra, Richards and Spencer Roads and part of Heeley City Farm) was adjacent to the perimeter of the Duke of Norfolk's Deer Park. Some of the field names indicate that before clearing the wooded areas had been harvested by coppicing to provide wood for fence and furniture making and also charcoal burning. Lady's Spring

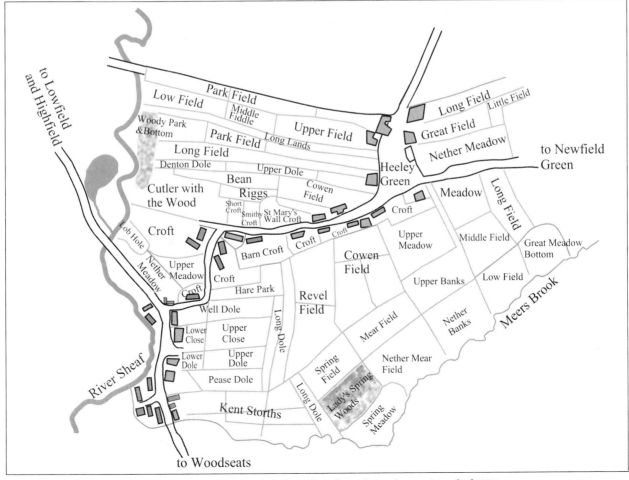

Field Names in a part of Heeley taken from the enclosure Award of 1791.

Wood was one such area used for this purpose. The trees would be lopped down to a stump initially and as new growth sprang up around the remnants of the old trunk it would be allowed to grow to certain widths and heights before harvesting. This wood was thus known as 'spring wood'. This is probably the origin of the name given to Springwood Road, rather than from the presence of water springs in the ground. David Hey states that *'most surviving broad leaved woods were coppiced for centuries up to about the First World war. Such woods had a characteristically different appearance from today for they were managed for underwood rather than mature trees. The cycle of years varied according to the product that was required … some underwood was cut in the first year of growth, but for pitprops the cycle was over 30 years.'*

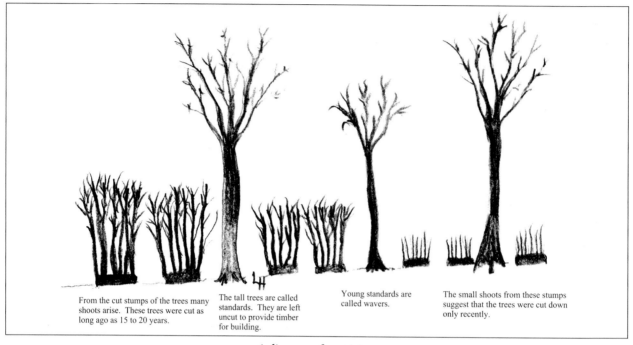

From the cut stumps of the trees many shoots arise. These trees were cut as long ago as 15 to 20 years.

The tall trees are called standards. They are left uncut to provide timber for building.

Young standards are called wavers.

The small shoots from these stumps suggest that the trees were cut down only recently.

A diagram of coppicing.

The Parliamentary Enclosure Act of 1791-1803 which awarded the remaining common pasture and open fields of Heeley to private landowners and freeholders did much to shape the development of Heeley in the nineteenth century.

The beneficiaries of the Enclosure Awards in Heeley included the following :-

Thomas Archdale	Sarah Atkin	Adam Broomhead	Rev James Wilkinson
John Bowden	George Bowden	Peter Brownell	Duke of Norfolk
Benjamin Broomhead	John Ash	Thomas Chapman	The Church Burgesses
John Gillott	John Hasland	James Kirkby	Twelve Capital Burgesses
William Marshall	Martha Nicholson	Samuel Shore	
George Woodhead	Philip Gell	Alexander Mackenzie	

The act provided for a forty foot wide road to run from the turnpike gate at Lower Heeley to pass Newfield Green and to be called Newfield Green Road (now Well Road and Gleadless Road) The road now known as Cat Lane was a private carriage road to Lees Hall. A footpath ran from the turnpike road at Lower Heeley to an ancient footway to Norton Lees.

Methodist services and Sunday Schools had been held in the open air or in people's homes since the 1770s. By 1826 land had been acquired for the building of a new Chapel and Sunday School, a building which is still in existence today. The Methodists not only saved their money to buy the stone and other materials for the building but actually built it themselves. The deeds of the chapel list many local tradesmen and cutlers who acted as trustees, some of whom can be picked out of the Directories of the time.

Jonathan Ackroyd	Mercer	Wm Fawley	Butcher
Edward Bailey	Cabinet Maker	Edward Gill	Cutler
James Bromley	Shoemaker	John Hasland	Cutler
Thos Brown	Gentleman	James Hodgson	Merchant
Geo Close	Cutler	Isaac Schofield	Cutler
Benjamin Denton	Grocer	Sam Hill Smith	Factor
Joshua Eyre	Grocer	William Staley	Merchant

HEELEY, *in Nether Hallam Township.*
Marked 1 live in Nether Heeley, 2 in Upper Heeley, 3 in Middle Heeley, & 4 in Newfield Green.

1 Askham Thos. warehouseman
2 Bagshaw T. vict. & shoemaker
1 Bailey Hannah, beerhouse
2 Barker Susanna, vict. Waggon and Horses
1 Bennett James, grinder
3 Birley Jph. earthenware dealer
2 Bolsover Mary, shopkeeper
3 Boot William, stone mason
1 Bradbury Thos. silver plater
1 Brailsford Mary and James, corn millers, Heely mill
1 Brandon Mr. Thomas
1 Brownell Rt. mert. *Newfield*
2 Gosling George, file mfr.
3 Gray Elizabeth, farmer
3 Hallatt Warrison, farrier
2 Hasland John, shopkeeper
2 Hawley Benj. file grinder
2 Hawley J. table knife grinder
4 Hollingworth Elias, farmer
4 Howe Joseph, shoemaker
2 Hydes William, schoolmaster
2 Jackson Wm. beerhouse
1 Kay John, shopkeeper
1 Kay John Sykes, grocer, &c.
1 Lowcock Jas. joiner & beerhs.
1 Makin Wm. file cutter
1 Marsden Jph. shoemaker
3 Marsden Richard, gardener
Naylor Joseph, cowkpr. Hick's ln.
1 Naylor Samuel, butcher
1 Ogden Jno. teapot handle mkr.
3 Parker Mary, horn button mfr.
Reynolds Geo, vict. White Lion
4 Rhodes Sydney, farmer
3 Scorah Rhoda, grocer & draper
3 Smith Jas. table knife mfr.
1 Stanley W. polishing paste mfr.
3 Swinscow David, beer house
3 Travis Henry, bookkeeper
1 Vardy Joseph, blacksmith and farrier
3 Vickers Charles, farmer
3 Ward William, vict. and tailor, Shakspeare
3 Wheatcroft John, merchant

1 White John, vict Red Lion
1 Wilson Isaac. shopkeeper
1 Wilson John, hat maker
Pocket Knife Manufacturers.
1 Archdale T.
2 Barlow Wm.
2 Beighton Geo
2 Gill Edward
2 Gill Stephen
2 Gillott David
2 Gillott Wm.
2 Hasland and Birley
2 Memmott G.
1 Memmott S.
2 Memmott W.
3 Palfreyman G.
2 Pemberton A.
2 Stones John
2 Taylor Thos.
2 Thompson C.
3 Wheatcroft L.
1 Wright Lear

> Some present members of the Heeley History Workshop are descended from **William Boot** and **G Palfreyman** mentioned in this extract

Excerpt from the White's 1833 Trade Directory.
Sheffield Local Studies Library

By 1830 Nether Heeley was a busy area with a main road from Sheffield coming into it and turning up Well Road to continue via Heeley Green and Newfield Green to Ford and Chesterfield and eventually London. In addition to the mill ponds, goyts and dams with their associated grinding wheels and trows, there was also file cutting and pen and pocket knife manufacture. File cutting especially could be done inside cottage homes or in cellar kitchens with large windows. White's Directory for 1833 lists eighteen pocket and pen knife manufacturers living in houses from Lower Heeley to Newfield Green and also 3 workers on files out of a total of only 64 householders. There were blacksmiths and other tradespeople, Public House landlords who often had a second job as well, shop-owners, farmers and a teacher for the Heeley National School on Heeley Green.

The area around the Shakespeare was now known as Middle Heeley – the term Upper Heeley being gradually pushed up the hill to the Heeley Green area. More and more trees were being cut down, more cottages and some terraced houses were being built in Lower Heeley. We know that stumps of felled oak trees (in the area of the present Oak Street) were used by local people as vantage points to watch soldier volunteers march by as they walked to Chesterfield en route for London and the Crimean War (1854-6).

"*An interesting ceremony took place at Heeley Parish Church on January 1st 1894, when Henry Stanley Granger was married to Alice Boot by the Rev. William Odom. This marriage between Mr. Granger and Miss Boot linked two farming families that were well known in Heeley; the Boot family lived in a farmhouse which had been erected sometime in the 1660's opposite the old Shakespeare Inn (on the site of where Oak Street Chapel was built); whilst the Grangers hailed from Myrtle Bank farm which was in what is now the Myrtle Road / Anns Road area. On his marriage certificate Henry Stanley Granger was said to be aged thirty four and his occupation was given as a tool maker, the address was the Farm, Myrtle Road, whilst his father was recorded as Joseph Granger, a cow keeper. Alice Boot was also aged thirty four, living at 219, Myrtle Road. and her father is given as William Boot (deceased) farmer. Witnesses to the wedding were Albert James Boot (a brother of the bride and also grandfather of Mrs Joyce Jenkinson of our Heeley History Workshop) and Mary Ann Granger (a sister of the bridegroom).*

Alice Boot

Henry Granger

Myrtle Bank Farm on Myrtle Road seems to have continued to exist even though houses in Myrtle Road and Anns Road surrounded it. Joseph Granger is listed as living there in 1893 as a coal and milk dealer and in 1894 as a cow keeper and 1895 as a cow keeper and milk dealer. By 1900 Mrs. Betsy Granger is listed as living at the farm, also as a cow keeper, but by 1905 it was a Mr. Smith there, whilst Henry Granger and his wife Alice were then living at 119, Myrtle Road.

In the middle of the nineteenth century Heeley was still very rural. In Middle Heeley apart from the Boot farm in the Oak Street, Sheaf Bank and Sheaf Street area there were also nurseries owned by Fisher Godwin in the Lower Heeley / Broadfield Road area and tenants of strip farming on the hillside area which became Spencer, Richards, Alexandra and Myrtle Roads. In the Heeley Bank area there were Rhubarb fields and strawberry fields. There were also many smallholdings or crofts and orchards associated with small messuages or dwellings. When one of our members talked to Mrs. Lawson and her sister (who were in their nineties and had lived in Myrtle Road all their lives); they recalled how they had seen the cows going from Myrtle Bank farm after the morning milking up the road to the fields in Upper Heeley beyond the top of Myrtle Road and then coming back down again for the early evening milking.

When widespread house clearance and demolition was carried out by the council in the late 1960's and early 1970's an area in the lower part of Spencer Road, Richards Road, Alexandra Road and Myrtle Road was designated as an inner city farm area. After considerable efforts land clearing and fund raising, the Heeley City Farm was established in the area and still exists today. The land occupied by this farm lies between the sites once occupied by the Boot farm and Myrtle Bank farm. We seem to have moved in a full circle, but it is ironic that the earlier farms were known as of Heeley, near Sheffield, whilst the farm today is described as an inner city farm. No doubt the earlier farmers if they could come back to visit today's farm would see very different breeds of animals to the ones which they handled." **Lilian Haywood**

Census Date	Population
1831	932
1841	1016
1851	1052
1861	2453
1871	7197
1881	8747
1891	11837

Population of Heeley from the census

As the population of Heeley increased from less than a 1000 in 1831 to ten times that by the end of the century there was a spate of building of terraced houses climbing up the hillsides from the valleys of the Meers Brook and River Sheaf. More places of religious worship were built to accommodate the population, the Anglican parish church, Christchurch, in 1848, Sheaf Street Primitive Methodist Chapel in August 1858, Heeley Wesley Chapel in October 1858 and Oak Street Wesleyan Reform Chapel in 1871. Some of the houses were occupied by people coming in from rural areas in Derbyshire, South Yorkshire or further afield.

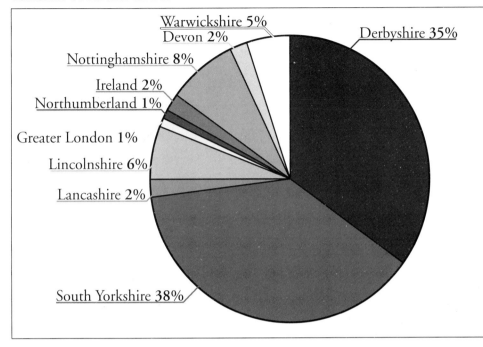

Birthplaces of persons listed in the 1851 census enumerators' books for Heeley but born outside Heeley of Sheffield

Total population 1052 including 117 from Sheffield and 268 from Heeley itself.

Some of these incomers still worked in Sheffield and travelled to work on the horse buses, later trams, but as work became increasingly available locally the men could walk home for a midday meal and be back before the afternoon buzzer went to restart work. During the 1870s and 1880s works opened up all round Heeley. Skelton's on Sheaf Bank, Hardy Patent Pick and Tyzack Sons and Turner on Little London Road all employed local men. Other Heeley workmen, little mesters and their workmen or those employed in the steel trade had a longer walk. Heeley Station opened in 1870 and some men travelled to Attercliffe, Tinsley and Brightside every day.

"My uncle Harry Gaunt and his father, my grandfather, worked for Arthur Lee's on the Sheffield-Rotherham border. They used to walk from home in Denmark Road to Heeley Station and catch the train to the nearest station in the East End. I think it was Brightside. Then they only had a short walk to work. The only snag was that they had to walk uphill all the way from the Station at the end of the day's work." **Joan Palfreyman.**

A tram on its way from town travelling along London Road, Heeley Bottom around the 1910s. *Sheffield Local Studies Library*

Mr Eddie Chapman at work at William Morton's in 1960

Memories of the cutlery trade, the main source of livelihood for Heeley people, come from days when jobs were easy to get and also from times of unemployment and hardship. The quotes below are the result of interviews by members of the Heeley History Workshop.

"Some local men shared rented workshops and worked as 'little mesters', doing outwork for city firms. Children took dad's dinner to t'shop in a basin where it was heated up on t'tortoise (stove)."

In the late 1800s and early 1900s cutlers were in great demand. With strong beer at eight pints to the shilling, some preferred drinking to working and bosses sometimes had to round up workmen from the pubs.

"When they got back to work in the majority of cases they were skint and first thing they would ask for would be a sub, (an advance on the payment for a job) and if they didn't give a sub, he would say, 'Well, what work am I to start on?' And of course the boss would give him a job out and he would sour that (he would draw on it straight away) if he possibly could. If a boss would let him he would draw it straight away before he started to work on it as a matter of fact." **HHW**

"On Monday, locally "St. Monday", 'sours' i.e. work paid for but not completed, were done in the morning, the afternoon being spent in the pub. Bosses might forget the sours, often never finished and hidden or thrown in the river." **Eddie Chapman**

Memories from between the wars are of cutlery as *"a mean trade, a very mean trade. Bosses were mean and they laid themselves open for anybody to get at them"*. 'Cuckoos', i.e. blades accounted for in the total of work done but returned for more satisfactory processing, were often purloined by the workmen and sold 'on the side'.

Women worked in the cutlery trade as well, some as burnisher's. *"You see, a burnisher could work at home because they didn't need machinery. But that was a woman's job; wasn't man's job, burnishing. And no girl could go into a factory, you know, where they did plates, silver plate and that sort of thing, no girl could go into that factory unless she said she wouldn't do any rough work at home. She wouldn't black lead, wouldn't wash pots, wouldn't do any scrubbing or anything like that, because her hands had to be so smooth, her skin' had to be so smooth that it didn't scratch the metal work. So of course quite a lot of the girls used to like it because it meant they had no work to do at home. Can't ask me to do the stair rods or black the stove or anything like that because I've got to have my hands soft for work."* **HHW**

Up to the Second World War many Heeley girls worked at buffing the heavy, dirty job of smoothing cutlery blanks on a buffing wheel. Rough girls, renowned through Sheffield, *"they were a breed of their own, they were a marvellous breed, you know, buffers."* During the war buffers were put on munitions work and few went back to buffing.

In the 1930s a firm's mark was etched on goods, exacting work involving the use of acid. At Viner's women got a shilling a gross for etching teaspoons and seven pence for three dozen best dessert spoons. At Tyzack's women were expected to etch heavy six-foot cross-saws.

"It was killing. We were nearly collapsing with the weight of them, and you know they are big teeth and you have got to be very careful as well. Well, it wasn't so bad if we could mix ours with some other work, but one day we had earned one shilling and sixpence between two of us, and you can imagine picking these six foot things up with the heavy pieces on each end that the handles used to fit in. So we struck, and we went down to the boss and we told him we were either leaving or we were not doing this, there were only two of us. We lost the job and they bought a rubber stamp that did it, but we had earned a shilling and sixpence between us." HHW

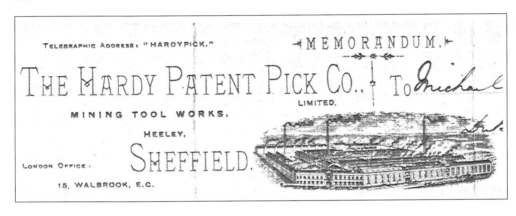

A memo heading from the offices of Hardy Patent Pick, one of Heeley's earliest large industrial works

By the 1930s the terrace housing had covered all the lower slopes of Heeley, except for part of Cutler's Wood and had extended up to Upper Heeley and Heeley Green. (see photo on inside back cover.)

"Those of us who spent a childhood in Heeley in the 30s first found it difficult to visualise Lower, Middle and even some parts of Upper Heeley as ever being rural. It seemed to consist of so many streets of small terrace houses full of people, big works with buzzers going four times a day, corner shops and house window shops in the middle of terraces. Apart from the buses that went up Heeley Green and the trams and trains on Heeley Bottom there were very few cars only horses and drays loaded with coal or fruit and vegetables. We did have daily reminders of local farms in the rounds of the farmers who had a horse and cart to deliver milk from a churn with a tap at the base. He would have a gill, half pint or pint measure to deliver the milk into a jug or basin. So depending on where we lived and before milk roundsmen from the pasteurising and bottling dairies took over you may have had milk deliveries from Ash Farm (near the Ball Inn), Heeley Common Farm (opposite the Prospect View), which was first Memmotts, then Waltons then Bradburys or from Newfield Green Farm or Lees Hall Farm or Armitage Farm on Farm Road or Lawsons Farm at the bottom of Hurlfield Hill. Newcombes in Lower Heeley, originally in Well Head Road (and even today in Artisan View) collected their milk churns from

Newfield Green Farm. *Sheffield Local Studies Library*

Heeley Station on special trolleys then delivered around Heeley from the same trolleys. On Albert Road Frank Wornell was noted for making his milk deliveries on a tricycle, going out from early morning to late lunch time on his morning round and late afternoon through evening for a second round. Langhorns had a shop at 24 Heeley Green from which he sold milk as did Jessops on Denmark Road/Bowler Street." **Lilian Haywood**

The greatest and most, spectacular fire in Sheffield's history occurred on Saturday night [April 23rd 1921] at the works of Messrs. C.T. Skelton and Co., Heeley, spade and shovel manufacturers.

"An inferno raged right on the edge of a highly congested area of worker's homes. A stiff dry wind fanned the flames and sparks. People were driven from their homes with their belongings - however, a plucky band of fire-fighters led by Superintendent Hadwick eventually got the fire under control. The cause of the fire is as yet unknown — 'no-one injured - 'thrilling' scene drew large crowds.

Albert Road in the 1960s with a delivery tricycle belonging to Frank Wornes known as 'Milky' outside the Crown. *Sheffield Local Studies Library*

The outbreak was discovered about 7.30 p.m. by George Ellis who alerted a passing police constable. The officer ran to the nearest telephone to inform the Fire Brigade. Superintendent Hadwick turned out with the 'Brigade. On arrival the centre of the huge section of the works which faces north and fronts the River Sheaf, was a mass of flames. Realising the dreadful possibility of an extension of the fire to Gleadless Road, he summoned further Brigade help. Soon nine machines including a motor fire pump and steamer were in action. The task seemed beyond them, the heat was terrific and it was decided to evacuate houses in the vicinity. At first people were content to rescue family valuables, but soon they were bringing out wringing machines, sideboards, tables and

The fire raging at Sketon's Sheaf Bank Works 1921 *Sheffield Local Studies Library*

all manner of things. Upper window frames were torn off and bedroom suites were passed down to helpers below, who rushed them away to safety. One householder even brought out his poultry. The roads were covered with red—hot charcoal, caps were pulled down over eyes and towels were wrapped round mouths.

The gallant and unceasing efforts of the firemen were finally rewarded - the houses and cottages were saved with the exception of no.6, Prospect View, the home of Mr. Thornton. His cottage roof was destroyed, but the main structure escaped serious damage. The two main buildings of the works were absolutely gutted, but although the timber yard caught fire, it was saved from complete destruction. The main forge, containing thousands of pounds worth of machinery, also escaped major damage.

About 7.30 p.m. Mr. Darley was standing on the concrete steps leading from his house which is inside the works, when he heard an explosion and saw flames spurt out from the third storey warehouse on the side of the works adjoining the railway line [it should be noted that the works are in a hollow and that the third storey is almost on a level with the line]. The warehouse was mainly stocked with small tools and contained no highly inflammable material apart from a small quantity of oil. Mr. Darley's home escaped with nothing more serious than the breaking of windows, although the house itself was within a few yards of raging masses of flame, that it had such a dramatic escape was entirely due to the skill and courage of the firefighters who successfully adopted an isolating policy.

Assisting at the fire were members of the Volunteer Fire Brigade, the Defence Corps, Royal Air Force men from Coal Aston, the Heeley members of the St. John Ambulance Brigade, Boy Scouts, ex soldiers, members of the works staff and many civilians. Their help was much appreciated by the Chief Constable, Colonel J. Hall-Dalwood and by Superintendent Hadwick. It was agreed that Skelton's fire was the biggest in living memory - the fire at Ranmoor Church was not on such a grand scale. Other fires called to mind, 1903, Pawson and Brailsford [Mulberry Street] and 1904, Black's Woodyard.

Skelton's fire took place on Cup Final day and it was estimated that more people watched the fire than attended the Final. It was said that the flames were seen as far away as Dronfield."
Alun Montgomery

After the blitz and the end of the war so many changes occurred, road transport increased considerably and there was felt by the City Council to be a need for new roads through Heeley. So many houses were pulled down and some businesses and some farms closed down. But the

An advertisement for Skeltons Sheafbank Works.

new roads were postponed, mainly for economic reasons and never built. From being a hive of industry and a warren of closely built housing Heeley became an area of much industrial and household rubble, with the employed commuting to work elsewhere and the unemployed wondering how to occupy their time. From part of this rubble the Heeley (Inner) City Farm was established in 1980, small industrial estates set up and a new Millennium Park established in stages (still incomplete) in the late 1990s.

Bomb damage on the corner of Richards and Prospect Roads.
Sheffield Local Studies Library

Looking across the Heeley Millennium Park towards Gleadless Road in 1999.

Pubs

In 1825 one of the earliest Trade Directories for 'Sheffield and Surrounding Villages' says that Heeley is divided into Upper Heeley, with Public House listings for the Ball Inn, the Wagon and Horses and the Shakespeare, and Nether Heeley with the Red and White Lions. All of these pubs are still trading one hundred and seventy-five years later although mostly in rebuilt premises. In the years since then the pub scene in Heeley has fluctuated as the population has changed with up to fifteen outlets open at one time.

Publicans in those days had other occupations as well; the landlords of the Ball have included a cutler, a file hardener and an edge tool grinder. Joseph Hawley of the White Lion is listed as a Blade Grinder in the 1841 census. Jobs such as these in local industry would have provided most of the income for the household, the pub would have been run by the man's wife or his son.

William Webster, landlord of the Shakespeare Inn from around 1854 to 1879 was listed as a Pocket Blade Grinder in the 1851 census living at Upper Heeley. In 1871 according to the census he was combining the trades of Innkeeper and Farmer. Following the history of one pub such as the Shakespeare through the Directories and census

HEELEY NETHER.

Archdale Thomas, pocket knife manufacturer
Binney and Brothers, Heeley Tilt, river Sheaf
Brailsforth John, corn miller, Heeley Mill
Brandon Thomas, victualler, White Lion
Close George, pocket comb manufacturer,
Jackson John, wood turner
Silcock Elizabeth, grocer
White John, victualler, Red Lion
Wright Lear, pocket knife manufacturer

HEELEY UPPER.

Barker George, Waggon and Horses
Barlow William, pocket knife manufacturer
Barlow William, pocket knife manufacturer
Binney John, pocket knife manufacturer
Bolsover James, pen and pocket knife manufacturer
Eadon Samuel, merchant
Gill Edward, pocket knife manufacturer
Gill Stephen,   do.   do.
Gillatt William,   do.   do.
Gillatt David,   do.   do.
Gillatt Thomas,   do.   do.
Gosling George, file manufacturer

Pemberton Thomas, pocket knife manufacturer
Robinson Mark, victualler, Shakespear
Stones James, pocket knife manufacturer
Stones Robert, pocket knife manufacturer
Thorpe William, victualler, Ball
Wheatcroft Luke, pocket knife manufacturer

Extracts from the 1825 Directory for Sheffield.
Sheffield Local Studies Library.

enumerators' books illustrates other aspects of the development of Heeley. In the excerpt shown from 1825 the Shakespeare is in Upper Heeley, by 1854 the area has been renamed Middle Heeley but it is not until 1871 that the first mention of a street name and number, 106 Gleadless Road, appears. This may have been a mistake on the part of the enumerator because in 1879 Well Road is given in a Directory. Apart from a brief straying into Oak Street in 1887 the pub's address remains 106 Well Road up to the present day.

In this picture the pub is shown by the name Ye Olde Shakespeare Inn, yet in the directories it is not listed by this name until 1954. All earlier listings give simply Shakespear, Shakespeare Inn or Shakespeare Tavern. David Fox, the present licensee will have served 40 years in March 2001.

The Shakespeare Inn around 1920.
Sheffield Local Studies Library.

The road through Heeley up to Newfield Green and on to Gleadless, Ford and Chesterfield had been the main route out of Sheffield to the south east until the building of the turnpike in 1756. The public houses along the way would have provided a change of horses and refreshment for the travellers.

The Waggon and Horses from a sketch. This building was demolished in 1882. Sheffield Local Studies Library.

"Joseph Berley was born in Heeley in 1806 and was an Edge Tool Grinder and Publican. His Beer House was in Lower Heeley before he moved on to the Old Waggon and Horses in Middle Heeley. He died there in 1849 at the age of 43 and his wife Mary took over the license until 1853 when she transferred it to her eldest son Henry. Henry died in 1865 at the age of 41 and joined his family in the local churchyard. The license was transferred to his younger brother, another Joseph, who had a coal yard opposite the pub. These buildings were on the site of the Heeley Green Cinema. The old pub was knocked down in 1882 and the new Waggon and Horses opened in 1883 with Joseph retaining the license. The date and his initials are on the arches over the door and one of the windows. He retired at the age of 64 and his family are in a double grave just inside the churchyard up the grassy slope to the right. The Old Toll Bar House which was opposite the Crown Inn at the bottom of Albert Road had the name J Berley over the door and a row of terraced houses on View Road were known as Berley Mount."

Sid Wetherill

The Waggon and Horses in the 1930s.

This picture was supplied by Mrs I Marsden whose parents (Mr and Mrs Bingham) were 'mine hosts' at the Waggon and Horses for thirty years. Mrs Marsden was the first baby to be born in the pub for over a hundred years.

The door in the corner is now a window

In 1830 a law was passed allowing premises to operate as Beerhouses, where the sale of spirits was not permitted. Dozens of new beer outlets opened all over Sheffield.

"I remember the words above such shops read, 'Licensed for the sale of ale, beer, porter and tobacco'"
Lilian Haywood.

Heeley leapt onto the bandwagon along with the rest of Sheffield and by 1834 three beerhouses were listed in the directories. Some of these would have been operated in the front rooms of houses and did not last the test of time but one purpose built establishment still open today was the Crown on Albert Road, named for the first time in 1856.

The Crown Inn on the corner of Albert and London Road.

Also given a name in this directory was the Bridge Inn at No 1 London Road South, although the present building only dates from the late 1930s. Many pubs were passed on in the family with a widow continuing to run the business after her husband's death until she remarried or a son was able to take over. The Ball changed hands when the widowed Mary Procter married Joseph Wood, a much younger man from Doncaster, around the late 1840s. The Waggon and Horses passed though several generations of Berley and the Bridge was run by three different members of the Gibbins family in the 1870s and 80s.

Next door to the Bridge was a row of shops, some on piers over the River Sheaf. In this picture these have already been removed. The present Bridge was built in a Tudor style and is set further back from the road.

In the distance the railway bridge passes over London Road just before the line reaches the station at Heeley.

The Bridge Inn shortly before it was rebuilt in 1937/8.
Sheffield Local Studies

The population of Heeley grew dramatically between 1851 (1,052 persons) and 1891 (11,837 persons) and the number of pubs in the area increased to keep pace. Some grocers' shops that had previously only sold beer by off licence, such as the Sheaf View Hotel and Station Inn, converted to beerhouses. By 1887 fifteen recognisable premises can be spotted in the directories although about half still did not have given names.

Pubs in Heeley
Shown on a plan traced from the Ordnance Survey map of 1906

Pubs

1. White Lion
2. Red Lion Hotel
3. Shakespeare Inn
4. Waggon & Horses
5. Ball Inn
6. Crown Inn
7. Bridge Inn
8. Myrtle Inn
9. British Oak
10. Sportsman Inn
11. Victoria Hotel
12. Newfield Inn
13. Prospect View Hotel
14. Sheaf View Hotel
15. Station Inn

Scale: 1/4 Mile

The Sheaf View Hotel can be traced through the census returns from its origins as a grocer's shop in 1871 under Hannah Blackford, a 72 year old widow, to its first mention as a Beerhouse in 1879 run by William Burley, later listed in the 1881 census aged 60. The running of this little business seems to have been a position for an older person at this time. But in 1891 Stephen Raynes is granted the licence by the Sheffield Magistrates and his age in the census is only 29 years. However Stephen is holding down another job too, as an Auctioneer's Clerk, so maybe the pub is being run by his wife?

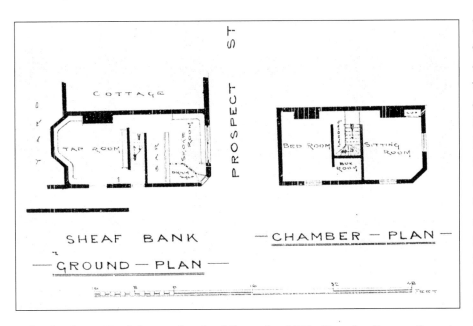

The Sheaf View Hotel from a plan dated September 1901. Note that Prospect Street is now known as Prospect Road. Sheffield Archives

In the plan here the layout of the tiny pub can be clearly seen. A Tap Room with a bay window looks out towards the River Sheaf, a Smoke Room and Dram Shop are served from the bar. Customers drinking in the Tap Room could enter through the door on Sheaf Bank, and must have been served by the landlord or his staff from the bar or even the cellar. In 1932 the current landlord was verbally cautioned by the police for allowing a betting slip to be written on his premises. It must have been hard for him to oversee the whole pub and presumably this was not the only time such a thing happened.

The pub was extended in the 1960s or 70s towards the river. Most people remember the extension as the pool or games room.

The Sheaf View has belonged to several breweries, Brampton Brewery in 1891 – does anyone know where this may have been? Then John Smiths of Tadcaster had the licence before the pub closed in the 1990s as a Marstons house. There seemed little hope of the pub reopening as the

The Sheaf View Hotel in 2000. James Birkett

houses round about had been demolished in the clearances of the 1970s and it was sadly boarded up for some years. But in 1999 James Birkett of the New Barracks Tavern, Hillsborough saw its potential and it reopened, completely refurbished as a real ale free house. The door into the old Smoke Room has been reopened on the corner of the pub but now leads into an airy L-shaped room, the original pub area makes a surprisingly narrow seating area and the bar has been moved to the far end into the old pool room.

Many of the newer beer outlets in Heeley have not been so lucky. After its change of use from a grocer's shop the Station Inn on London Road sold beer on the premises for only a few years and was lost when the railway bridge over London Road was widened in the 1890s.

Source	Date	Address	Forename	Surname	Age	Occupation/Trade Category/Owner
Census	1861	5 London Road	Samuel	Drury	33	Gentleman Servant Provision Dealer
Census	1871	5+7 London Road	William R	Richardson	26	Grocer and Beerseller
Trade Directory	1887	5 London Road	Charles	Hand		Beer House
Licensing Records	8 Sep 1887	London Road	Henry	Spencer		Midland Railway Co
Census	1891	5 London Road South - Station Road	Henry	Spencer	48	Publican
Trade Directory	1893	515 London Road South	Henry	Spencer		Beer House
Licensing Records	1901		Henry	Spencer		Licensed not renewed

Extracts from the census, trade directories and licensing records for the Station Inn, Heeley.

Three pubs around Lower Heeley, the Myrtle, the Sportsman (or Boiler's Rest) and the British Oak were lost to the house clearances of the 1970s in readiness for a new road that was never built.

A grassy bank between Alexandra and Myrtle Roads opposite the Heeley City Farm is all that remains of where the Myrtle stood. Although named the Myrtle, interestingly the address of the pub was always 33 Alexandra Road but a narrow passageway did lead through onto Myrtle Road from its rear. It was licensed for billiards, music and dancing but an entry in the Magistrates Records shows the licensee was cautioned for allowing cards to be played. Along with several other pubs in the area the pub fell foul of the Lighting Order of 1916, a 'black out' ruling to prevent air raids during the First World War. The licensee was fined 40/- or £2 in today's currency.

The British Oak stood on Oak Street, on the opposite side to the United Reform Methodist Chapel but lower down the road nearer to London Road. It appears to have begun its life as a front room Beerhouse at 30 Oak Street, run firstly by Thomas Biggin, a File Forger and then by his surviving widow Mary after Thomas died in 1865. Around 1876 the building was rebuilt or extended and is listed with the address 28 & 30 Oak Street thereafter. Still run by a dual occupation landlord the licensee in 1881 is a Joiner's Tool Maker and in 1891 a Jobbing Grinder. The tradition of passing the pub on to a widow appears to be repeated in the 20th century when Bertha Walker is listed as the licensee from 1948, the licensee from 1924 had been Frank Bruce Walker. The pub is remembered as long, narrow and rather dark with a snooker table.

Oak Street in 1966 showing the British Oak on the right.
Sheffield Local Studies Library.

The Sportsman Inn on Whit Sunday 1950s.

At the top of Oak Street on its junction with Well Road stood the Sportsman Inn. Commonly known as the Boiler's Rest it supposedly gained this name when a large boiler, intended for a laundry business fell from the cart on which it was being transported up Gleadless Road, rolled down the hill and came to a sudden stop embedded in the wall of the pub. No-one is now sure of the site of the laundry, but the event appears to have occurred in 1893, certainly the alternative name is recorded in the Magistrates Records in Sheffield Archives which date from 1896. Listed as a pub in the 1871 census it seems likely that it was purpose built, the picture shows a sizeable white corner pub with beers from the Henry Tomlinson Brewery.

The Prospect View Inn (or Cuckoo) which had been at 500 Gleadless Road on Heeley Common was demolished at around the same time as the previous three in Lower Heeley. Set in the middle of a row of terrace houses the pub was mounted on the edge of Gleadless Road overlooking a steep drop into the Meers Brook valley. It was the only one on the block to have a front and a back entrance. It also had its share of dual occupation landlords being the home of a millwright in 1881 and a pocket knife cutler in 1891. One family, the Oldfields, appear to run the pub from 1895 to its demolition with John Henry being followed by Henry and then Annie. The beers were from T Rawson and Co and although it started life as a Beerhouse by 1938 it enjoys a full listing in the Directories as a Public House.

Several pubs built to service the growing population of Heeley survive until the present day although their surroundings are somewhat changed. The Newfield Inn on Denmark Road is first listed in a Trade Directory in 1864 and the Victoria is listed in the 1871 census. Named the Roundhouse for the distinctive shape of the frontage, the pub has survived the many changes in the road layouts in the area. The Victoria now stands on the corner of Farish Place and Gleadless Road whilst Heeley Green has been cut off from the site by the rerouting of Richards Road.

The Victoria, a Ward's pub until the brewery closure in 1999.

On London Road, the main route out of Sheffield towards Chesterfield, the pubs have survived much better. The Bridge has already been mentioned as a survivor although rebuilt and the Station as a loss when the railway bridge was widened but beyond the bridge the White and Red Lions are still holding on. In fact a new licensed premises, the Easy Street, opened in 2000 in several combining refurbished shop buildings between the two Lions.

The White Lion has an interesting display of its history mounted on the walls of the pub and the front part of the interior has to be seen to be properly appreciated. Several small rooms, almost like cabins lead off a narrow corridor with the bar on the left fronted by a small snug. Although unfortunately opened out at the rear the pub still has many interesting features.

The joke amongst the members of the Heeley History Workshop is that there was once a Blue Lion on London Road too. Innocent researchers trying to pin this one down are then informed that they suppose it doesn't really count as it was a Temperance Bar!

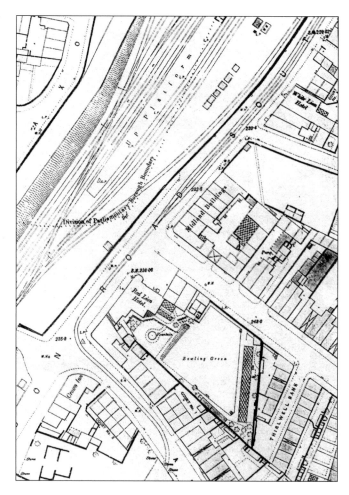

Ordnance Survey Map of Heeley from 1891.
Sheffield Local Studies Library

The Red Lion figures in one of the most famous pictures of Heeley and has appeared in many previous local history books. The pub was the terminus for the early horse bus service to Heeley starting in 1854 which provided a cheap form of transportation for the working men so that they could live in the more healthy air of Heeley and yet travel into work each day in Sheffield. Later the terminus for the horse tram, the tram sheds still exist in Albert Road just around the corner. Our picture has been chosen to show the pub one hundred years later in the 1950s, tram wires still above the roads and an old police box in place on the corner of Thirlwell Road. The advertising on the side of the White Lion can just be glimpsed down the road.

There are eleven licensed premises in Heeley today.

London Road in the 1950s. Sheffield Local Studies Library.

Churches

Heeley Church Institute, Gleadless Road, the first place of Christian worship built in Heeley and now a listed building, opened as a Wesleyan Chapel in 1826. The conveyance of the land, which cost £16.13.4, was signed on July 15th 1826 by four men of Heeley and eleven men of Sheffield. At this time Heeley was still predominantly rural. In the Sheffield Directory of 1833 Heeley is described as, "the populous village of Upper and Nether Heeley, nearly two miles south of Sheffield." Much later, Canon Odom in his book 'Fifty Years of Sheffield Church Life 1866 – 1916', comments on the rural character of the chapel's surroundings as he describes his first visit to the Chapel in the 1860's:

"A lady friend from the country desired to hear the Reverend John Gutteridge, a noted Free Methodist minister, who was announced to preach in the old Chapel (now used as a club room), by the corner of the churchyard. On my undertaking to be her guide, we went up a narrow lane with old farm buildings at the top (now Oak Street), until we reached Gleadless Road, where all was open country and gardens. As I sat in the small crowded Bethel, little did I dream that the day would come when I should be the vicar of the adjoining church, privileged to minister amidst a population of nearly 18,000 souls."

Heeley's First Methodist Chapel, built 1826

This small chapel became a hive of religious activity; enhancing and bringing joy and happiness into the hard lives of the local folk who in those early days could be accommodated within its walls. The Word was expounded faithfully, often in open-air services. The Anniversary of the chapel and Sunday school, the annual Charity Sermon, the Whitsuntide Treat and the Social Tea at Christmas were red-letter days. When the foundation stone of the parish church was laid on November 4th 1846, members of the chapel gave a treat to the Sunday school scholars to celebrate the event.

The Parish Church of Christ Church, Heeley, arose out of the vision of one man, the Reverend Henry Farish who wished to establish a Church in Heeley, an area hitherto rural, but of rapidly growing population. He was the Vicar of St Mary's, Bramhall Lane, which had opened in 1830 and, so far as the established Church was concerned, had the people of Heeley in his care. At this time, the only place of Christian worship in the vicinity was the small Wesleyan Chapel which had opened in 1826 and which still stands at the junction of Hartley Street and Gleadless Road. Already during the years of 1844 and '45, Henry Farish had been holding two meetings a week in people's homes. On the occasion of his second marriage in 1845, the congregation of St Mary's resolved to help him realise his vision by collecting subscriptions as a gift towards the building of such a church and the Church Burgesses provided the present site in Gleadless Road.

The foundation stone was laid on November 4th 1846, and the church – built to accommodate 450 people – was erected over the next two years at a cost of £2,695. It was consecrated in August 1848 by Archbishop Musgrave of York. The service was attended by many notable Sheffield residents, including the local poet and hymn writer, James Montgomery, and the Reverend Henry Farish preached the sermon.

Christchurch, Heeley with the Methodist chapel in the foreground, sketch dated 23rd June 1893.
Sheffield Local Studies Library.

The original church was cruciform in shape with a tower about sixty feet in height over the north transept on which it was intended to add a spire, but this was never done.

The first vicar was the reverend Henry Denson Jones, formerly Chaplain at Sheffield Infirmary, who was to minister here for forty-two years. As yet no vicarage house had been built near the church and Denson Jones for a time lived at Highfield House (near where the present Highfield Library stands today), where he could look across the valley of the Sheaf and see his Church of Christ, standing proudly on the hillside of Middle Heeley. However, in1862 he moved to the substantial vicarage, which was built near the church at a cost of £1,500. During his long ministry, Denson Jones had seen what was a predominantly rural population in Heeley increase by thousands, many of whom were engaged in industry. In the end, with increasing age and failing physical and mental health, he was no longer able to cope with the exacting demands of his ministry and the changing situation. He resigned in 1888, and died in 1894 at the age of eighty. Henry Denson Jones was buried in Heeley churchyard. His gravestone, much eroded by time, may still be seen today to the west of the porch of the church, which he had served for so long.

Henry Denson Jones' successor was William Odom, a remarkable man, who was Vicar of Heeley Parish Church from 1888-1816. On offering him the parish of Heeley in 1888, Dr Thomson, the Archbishop of York at that time said, 'I feel sure that the parish would fare well in your hands,' and William Odom was to justify this faith. Under his leadership the church witnessed a tremendous growth in the number of souls attending and the successful introduction of a number of organisations and activities of a religious, social and educational nature. To accommodate these he and his congregation embarked on a building extensions programme which completely transformed the physical appearance of the church and its immediate surroundings.

In 1889, early in his ministry, he introduced the first parish magazine that became a popular feature in the parish; thousands were sold! If parishioners wished the year's magazines were bound in a stiff-backed volume at a cost of 1d a magazine. Even today these volumes are a mine of information about the Heeley of his day.

"For several months we have rented three large rooms in Gleadless Road Board School at the rate of £20 per annum. Now it is felt that the time has come when an effort should be made to erect a large room on the upper part of the land secured to the Church some time ago. Respecting the land, which had it not been secured by the vicar would now have been covered with cottage houses it may be said that it was purchased at a cost of £230, towards which, £100 is at hand. The land, which has a frontage of 120 feet to Hartley Street, adjoins the churchyard and forms one of the best possible sites for Sunday School buildings. The Parish Church Sunday School teachers have already considered and approved the matter and promised to do all they can to collect subscriptions. Fill in the Subscription Form in this magazine and in the name of Christ and for the sake of our children, return it before June 20th 1893, forward a subscription, however small."

On Friday evening May 12th, the Parish Church Council met in the Church room when the vicar stated the pressing need for additional Sunday School accommodation and produced plans and estimates showing that a new and substantial brick building could be put up for about £320. As to funds, he thought that at least half this amount could be raised before the end of the year by small subscriptions, collecting books etc.. The large

The Sunday School Rooms on Hartley Street, demolished in 1999.
Sheffield Local Studies Library.

room would be built first and extensions could be made as required. The council welcomed the idea of a brick building and firmly rejected a suggestion that a corrugated iron room would do instead. It was further suggested that part of the new building should be used for the Young Men's Bible Class and a weekday Institute and Reading Room. The meeting adjourned to Wednesday 31st of May, having unanimously approved the proposed plans. It was hoped that a start on the building could be made that same summer

The church itself was enlarged in 1890 when the nave was lengthened by one bay, a new aisle built on the north side providing 320 more 'sittings', and an organ chamber were added at a cost of £1,750. The architect was Mr JD Webster. The church was reopened on May 16th, 1890 by Archbishop Thomson of York, who preached his last sermon in Sheffield at the service before his death later in the year. The Sunday School, again the architect was JD Webster, was officially opened on November 30th 1893 by the new Archbishop of York, Dr McLagan, who on the same day held a confirmation, the first held in Heeley Church, where 110 candidates (83 from the parish) were confirmed.

In 1896 to commemorate the Golden Jubilee of the church it was resolved to raise £1,200 to complete the extension of the church by the addition of a south aisle which would seat a further 140 persons. Memorial stones were laid by Mrs Blakeney and Miss Leila Roberts who acted on behalf of her aunt, Miss Roberts of Park Grange who was ill. These stones bearing the initials MB and JR are clearly seen embedded in the south wall today. The extension was duly completed and the church reopened in June 1897.

In March 1913 William Odom was saddened by the sudden death of his wife Mary, she had been his devoted helper and companion for thirty-five years. Sadly missed by the parishioners they donated and installed the beautiful stained glass window in the east end of the church in her memory.

At the Easter Vestry Meeting of 1916 the Revd. Odom announced his intention to retire. At the age of 70 he felt it was time to make way for a younger man. He preached his last sermon on the last Sunday in October that year, his successor being the Revd Edwin Arthur Miller. The text for his sermon 'Jesus Christ, the same yesterday and today and forever', (Hebrews 13:7,8) was the very text which

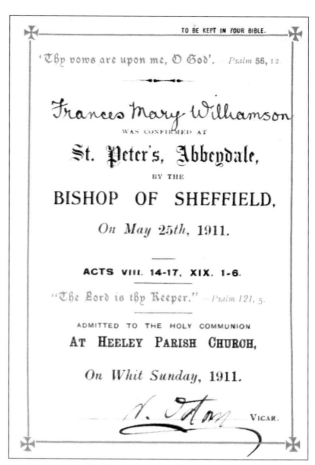

Confirmation card from 1911,
signed by William Odom.

for many years successive congregations could read for themselves over the main arch of the church. Heeley was always to remain dear to the Canon and his mortal remains are with us still. He lies buried beside his wife in a grave not far from the church he loved. The Heeley of today is vastly different from the Heeley of Canon Odom's day, but his name lives on in Odom Court opposite the church.

As the nineteenth century progressed and the population of Heeley grew, becoming increasingly engaged in industry, churches of other denominations were opened in the area, joining in the work of evangelism of which the 1826 chapel had been the pioneer. In 50 years no fewer than eleven centres of worship were established in the Heeley/Meersbrook area. Oak Street, Anns Road, Heeley Wesley, Valley Road, Kent Road and Meersbrook Bank were all opened by 1898. The remainder were Christchurch, Heeley Friends, St Peter's Mission Church, Meersbrook Congregational Church and the Salvation Army.

Memorial card from 1915, signed by William Odom.

About 1850 the Methodist Reform Movement, which was growing nationally, was becoming very strong in Heeley. 'Splinter' groups, discontented with developments in the Methodist Conference, were formed. Eventually, however, the Reformers Committee, at a quarterly meeting at Norfolk Street, consented to the "seceders" taking over the first chapel building with its liabilities of about £200. Robert Hey describes the formation of the United Methodist Free Church in Heeley in 1857 by an amalgamation of the Reform Methodists and the Wesleyan Methodist Association. They remained in the old building until a new chapel was built on Oak Street in 1871.

The Oak Street Chapel, built 1871, burnt down 1946, with the lecture room, originally part of Boots' Farm to the right.
Sheffield Local Studies Library.

"In the minutes of December 1864 it is recorded that a deputation form the Chapel Trustees of the school declared their intention to take preliminary steps to build a Chapel which should be an ornament to the village. They promised to provide for the secular as well as the religious education of the children of Heeley. … The purchase price [of the land] was £200 for 1,000 sq yards, further land was bought in 1871, 1887 and 1903 amounting to 3,512 sq yards. … On March 26th 1971, the Reverend Gutteridge, a former minister, preached at the opening service. … They had a membership of 477 and 59 juniors. … Electric light was installed in the Oak Street Chapel in 1922 at a cost of £212 and in 1926 with the co-operation of the vicar of Heeley, the Rev AE Duckett and the Ministers of the other churches in Heeley we celebrated the centenary of the opening of the little Chapel in Gleadless Road. A gathering of about 5,000 people assembled in the open air at the corner of Hartley Street and Gleadless Road and the singing was conducted by Sir Henry Coward."
H K 1928

The Oak Street premises were gutted by fire in December 1947 and the members worshiped in nearby Anns Road Church until on 1st December 1948 they were linked together to form one church, renamed St Andrew's.

The immediate forefathers of the Methodist Church in Anns Road first met for worship in the home of Mr Richard Tomlinson in Oak Street in 1857. They opened the second Methodist Chapel in Heeley on 8th August 1858 at the bottom of Gleadless Road (then called Sheaf Street).

Sheaf Street Chapel, firstly home to the Primitive Methodists then to St Leonards Church.

Criticus, a local writer for the Sheffield newspapers, described Primitive Methodistsas "vigorously independent and firmly artisan." Their chapel in Heeley, on Sheaf Street was one of 31 built between 1840 and 1880 mostly amongst the newly developed areas of working class streets springing up around Sheffield. The Sheaf Street Chapel and Sunday School flourished and by the 1890's the congregation there had decided to build a much larger chapel to accommodate their growing numbers. The site chosen was on Anns Road and in 1897 they moved up to this new Primitive Methodist Chapel, a much more splendid building than the former. The building was taken over in the same year (1897) by the Salvation Army where it became the centre of their work amongst the poor and needy of Lower Heeley.

At the end of the 1920s the Sheaf Street Chapel came into the possession of the parish church of Christ Church, Heeley when it was purchased during the Vicariate of the Reverend AE Duckett in the 1920's, and so became St Leonard's, the daughter church of Heeley Parish Church. St Leonard's continued to thrive during the ministry of his successor, the Reverend William Kendall. Many services were held there, including a Children's Church. Missionary meetings were held for children aged eight to fourteen, where magic lantern slides of missionary work in Africa and the East were shown and plays occasionally performed by the children in Eastern dress. A Children's Operetta Society was later set up under the direction of the Reverend A Smith, a curate at the parish church. As the Men's Bible Class grew in number, it was moved from the Church Institute to St

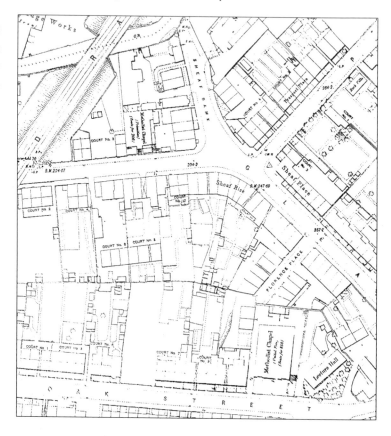

Ordnance Survey Map of 1891 showing Sheaf Street and Oak Street Chapels. Sheffield Local Studies Library

Leonard's. It was very popular and became the biggest in the Deanery, at one time numbering over 120 members and having a small orchestra to lead the singing. It was also the venue for the Girl Guides, Rangers and Women's Own.

The Second World War and its aftermath, however, were soon to adversely affect the spiritual life of the community of Heeley and its religious institutions, and St Leonard's was no exception. During the Vicariate of the Reverend Donald Howe (1948 – 53) it was reluctantly decided that it was no longer practical to continue to maintain a daughter church so close to the mother church when all its activities could be incorporated into the life of the parish church itself. Much to the regret of its faithful congregation, St Leonard's was closed and the building sold. This sturdy old building has withstood the test of time, but its walls no longer echo to the sound of hymn or prayer. In an age more materialistic that its heyday, it is now used for commercial purposes and is a printing firm. St Leonard's, Norfolk Park, which opened in the 1960's and was until recently a daughter church of Christ Church, Heeley, was so named to commemorate the first St Leonard's.

The Anns Road premises were built to cater for the expanding needs of the Primitive Methodists in their Sheaf Street Chapel. It was opened in the spring of 1897, the architect was Mr J Taylor and the structure, exclusive of land, cost £5,000. At that time the church had a membership of 200 and 250 Sundays School scholars with 47 Sunday School teachers. Held in the new building were the Band of Hope, the Literary Society, Mother's Meetings and Mission Bands. The choir of the church was one of the 'best voluntary choirs in Sheffield'.

"Anns Road Chapel Schoolroom was opened on the morning of the 13th of December 1940 as a Rest Centre for those whose homes had been destroyed in the Sheffield Blitz. The Centre was supplied with bunks and field kitchens were erected in the school yard opposite. More than 300 people lived for several days on the premises, their needs being cared for by a staff of willing volunteers. The annual performance of 'The Messiah' should have been given on Sunday 15th December but instead the bottom of the chapel was full of homeless folk who sang their favourite hymns as

Ann's Road Church, later St Andrew's from the Jubilee Booklet, 1947.

the Schoolroom was cleaned. The WVS personnel attached to the Centre were, for the most part, members of the Church, and the work was so efficiently carried out by them, that Anns Road was the last centre to close, homeless from other Centres being transferred to our Centre as their numbers were decreased by billeting. Their Majesties, the King and Queen, [George VI and the present Queen Mother] visited the City during January 1941 and we were all proud when Ann's Road was the Centre chosen for them to inspect. When flying bombs started falling on London and it became necessary to evacuate many women and children, the Ann's Road Centre was again brought into operation, this time, to care for the welfare of over 380 panic-stricken women and children." From the Anns Road Methodist Church Jubilee Souvenir Booklet, 1947.

The Chapel closed in 1990 and the building now houses the privately run Bethany School and Chinese Christian Church.

Further building in Heeley was carried out by the Wesleyan Methodists. This was another splinter group of the old Methodist Society who broke away in the 1840s and 50s. A pamphlet was written to celebrate the centenary in 1927 of the Brunswick circuit, to which Heeley Wesley belonged. Remember in reading this extract that the author was, no doubt, heavily biased towards his own version of Methodism.

"The little Methodist community in the scattered and picturesque village of Heeley found themselves as sheep without a shepherd after the closing down of the old Chapel in Gleadless Road in the late forties. This Chapel was built in 1826 and did remarkable work in its day. Having no permanent spiritual home the Methodist folk were compelled to hold open-air services in a tent on Thirlwell Bank in a field below Thirlwell Terrace, the scene of periodic gypsy encampments. In addition to this handicap, Methodism had to fight for its life against Reform agitation, which was vigorously prosecuted in Heeley about the year 1855 and found its resources considerably weakened. However the faithful few held on, and in September 1857 the decision to build a Chapel at Heeley was approved ... the foundation stone was laid

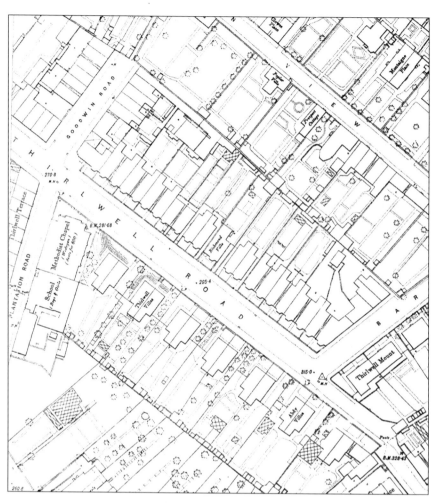

Ordnance Survey Map of 1891 showing part of Thirlwell Road. Sheffield Local Studies Library

on May 17th 1858 by Mr William Cockayne and the Chapel was opened on October 20th 1858. The work flourished. In 1859 tract distributors had mapped out the village and people came and filled the church. An

The corner of Thirlwell Road and Plantation Road in 1966. Sheffield Local Studies Library.

enlargement was necessary ... on April 17th 1865 the foundation stone of the large schoolroom was laid. In 1872 Wesley Chapel was enlarged again by the addition of two side aisles and the erection of three galleries and two new vestries. This increased the seating accommodation to 550. The first marriage was solomnized [in the chapel] on April 2nd 1872."

Extracts from the Centenary of Brunswick Circuit, 1927 in Local Pamphlets, Sheffield Local Studies Library.

The chapel is now a Mosque.

St Peter's Mission Church was founded by Mr Charles Crute in 1880 housed in a corrugated iron roofed building at the back of Richards Road. During the 1880s the vicar of Heeley, the Rev Denson Jones, was becoming old and infirm and was reluctant to take on the care of the mission church. When Rev Odom came to Heeley in 1889 he agreed to help and friends from the mission church guaranteed £100 per annum towards pastoral help for the mission. This link did not last long as notice was given that the land was needed for housing and there was despair that the mission would have to close. Mr JD Cook who lived in Meersbrook then provided a site in Fitzroy Road and the foundation stones of the new church were laid in 1895. On October 17th 1897 the Sunday School opened for services and the church was opened for public worship before the end of the same year.

"I remember … The people walking to church in hundreds, and the sound of the congregation singing coming through the open door. The church bell would start to ring about ten o'clock and would cease about twenty-five minutes past ten it was a single bell and its sound was Dong, Dong, Dong, with a slight hesitation between when the ringer got a bit tired. Whitsunday sounds were different from any other Sunday in the year, the children bubbling with excitement making their way to Sunday school to collect their ticket for the bun and coffee on Whitmonday afternoon, (only those who attended regularly got a ticket although some managed to get away with it). On Whitmonday morning the children and the teachers would assemble outside Sunday school and after singing there, the band bugles and drums, with the Sunday school banner leading the way, would march up Gleadless Road, Penns Road, singing again at the corner of Denmark Road and Penns Road, down Denmark Road to the junction of Heeley Green, then down Heeley Green to be joined then with the children from Heeley Friends, Anns Road, Oak St., all with their bands and banners, down to Heeley Bottom to be joined by Ebenezer and Heeley Wesley and other churches. The hundreds of people lining the route,

Sunday School Banner 1950s

all calling to the children, and proudly marching to the Park in their Whitsunday best. The friends and relatives all talking happily together. The big drum banging away, and children being lifted on the platform who had got lost. The buns and coffee in the afternoon after the races the children racing in their various ages excited the parents shouting them on. If the wind was in the right direction you could hear the singing in Heeley from Meersbrook Park." **Eddie Chapman aged 98 in 2000 who attended St Peter's Church and Sunday School.**

The building is now occupied by the Heeley Church of the Nazarene.

Whitsuntide was also remembered by another member, Alf Cooke.

"Easter and Whitsuntide were Church festivals which were celebrated in the open air. On Easter Sunday afternoon, the choir, Sunday School and congregation assembled in the Churchyard to take part in a Resurrection Service. At Whitsuntide there was more activity. The children who attended the Sunday Schools went to the schoolrooms for breakfast on Whit Monday morning and then processed to Meersbrook Park, where all the nonconformist Sunday Schools of the area assembled to sing Whitsuntide Hymns. Heeley Church did not join the Chapels, but paraded through the parish, led by the choir, the uniformed organisations etc. stopping at various road junctions to sing hymns. In the afternoon, the children assembled at Church and walked to Lawsons' field (just beyond what is now the Newfield Green shopping centre) to join in games and races and most of all to enjoy a paper bag containing sandwiches and buns."

The old 1826 chapel, small as it was, continued to serve the community in various ways. In 1874 the Heeley Wesley chapel rented the "Old Chapel in Gleadless Road" for use as a "young men's school", according to the late AW Booker, probably as a Sunday school. Then during the 1880's and 1890's the building was used as a day school on weekdays (see page 7). For a time the chapel also became the meeting place for the Liberal Club.

On September 5th 1926 an open-air united service which was held to celebrate the centenary of its opening, when Mr Henry Kirk of Oak Street Methodist referred to, *"the mighty faith and courage of our forefathers in building this church."* Over five thousand people attended the service which was held in the open, outside the building. The churches represented were Heeley Parish Church, Heeley Wesley, Oak Street United Methodists, Ann's Road Primitive Methodists, St Peter's Mission Church, Kent Road Primitive Methodists, and the Salvation Army. The Vicar of Heeley, the reverend AE Duckett presided and the Reverend LJ Hunt, minister of Heeley Wesley, gave the address.

In 1976 another open-air service celebrating the hundred and fiftieth anniversary of its opening was held in Hartley Street and was conducted by the Reverend Alan Homer, Vicar of Heeley. With the passing of time the date 1826 above the doorway has been eroded, but as a building it still stands solidly, much as it did so many years ago. Though no longer a place of worship, all may not be lost: at the time of writing there are plans to restore this building, one of the few remaining monuments to Heeley's past, so that it may once again serve the people of Heeley.

Whitsun Parade outside Oak Street Chapel. *Sheffield Local Studies Library.*

Childhood and Schools

Heeley in the eighteenth century was a small village surrounded by farmlands and woodland and the poor children would have to take their place in the fields, so education was almost non-existent.

In 1801 a building stood on common land in Upper Heeley which was used as a school. The National School was built with an endowment of about £14 per annum, the chief benefactor being a Mr. Thomas Chapman who died on 19th June 1801, at, the age of 81 years. Canon Odom gave an explanatory resume of Heeley National School in "Fifty Years of Church Life". The site of the present buildings (5,208 square yards) was purchased from the Lord of the Manor by subscription. In 1809 the master was instructed to teach church catechism. In 1833, the school was enlarged by subscription from trustees who, in 1838, numbered eleven, including several well-known Heeley names. In 1841, in addition to "pay scholars" eighteen others were taught free. A further extension and a house for the headmaster were built in 1868.

A set of rules was given to the parent or guardian of prospective students.

Rules of Heeley Pay Schools in 1843 extracted from Canon Odom's Book

1. Each child on first coming to school is to pay twopence, which sum is to be paid regularly in advance early Monday morning. For this will be taught reading, writing and arithmetic and to the girls needlework.

2. The school hours are from Lady Day to Michaelmas, in the morning from 9 a.m. to twelve noon and in the afternoon from 2 p.m. to 5 p.m. From Michaelmas to Lady Day, in the morning from 9 a.m. to twelve noon and in the afternoon from 1.30 p.m. to 4 p.m.. On Sunday throughout the year at 9 a.m. in the morning and at 2.p.m. in the afternoon.

3. Children are to be sent neat and clean and the girls without necklaces, feathers or finery.

4. It is expected that no child be kept from school without leave being granted the day before. Children whose attendance is irregular after repeated admonitions will be dismissed. If any child be detained at home by illness the parents are expected to acquaint the master.

5. If any child behave ill at school, or be idle and careless in doing what is set them, they will be detained after school hours.

6. Parents who intend to withdraw their children are expected to give previous notice to the Master of the school.

7. Work will be provided for girls two days in the week. On other days they may bring their own work, only fancywork will not be allowed.

8. The presence of the children on Sundays is required in order that they may receive religious instruction and attend church.

9. Any child living In Upper or Lower Heeley may be admitted, provided the parents agree to conform to the above rules.

10. When a child is brought for the first time, one of the parents or guardians of the child is required to come and consent to the rules and receive a copy of them, after which the Child's name may be enrolled.

11. Children attending the Sunday School and not the day school are required in all respects to submit to the discipline of the school and to attend church under the conduct and guidance of the Master.

The building still stands today, though at the time of writing it is empty.

Heeley National School, endowed 1801. One of the oldest buildings in Heeley.

Extracts from the Heeley National School Logbook.

(Mr Thomas Howick Headmaster)

December 2nd 1862	Mr Mitchell from the Sheffield School of Art examined this school in State Drawing and awarded prizes to Marion Howick, Clara Spry, M Fidler, G Memmot, R Brown and GA Barker.
July 7th 1863	Heeley nuisance, commonly called Heeley Feast, school badly attended.
July 27th 1863	Gate day at the Botanical Gardens. The Sheffield people are too fond of holidays keeping the children excited and schoolwork is neglected.
August 7th 1863	Louisa Gregory in the 4th class was seized with cholera, died in about 24 hours.
August 10th 1863	Wm Whaley of 3rd class died last night of scarlet fever after a short illness. A nice boy and making good progress, several cases of fever.
August 31st 1863	Harvest having commenced the attendance not so good as usual.
October 23rd 1863	A fine day, several children absent this afternoon getting blackberries.
January 4th 1864	School reopened today, scanty attendance, very sharp frosty weather, children late.
February 17th 1864	Mr Flockton's men came this morning to take the dimensions of the schoolroom and Mr Roberts called about the plan for the classroom.
March 14th 1864	Many children absent today, gone to Sheffield to see the devastation caused by the flood which happened in the night between 11 & 12 inst. Awful! Calamity!!

The Education Act of 1870 saw a change in education. School Boards were introduced for the education of children between the ages of five and thirteen years. Sheffield's board was elected on November 28th 1870. The building of Lowfields School was started in 1872, but due to building difficulties was not completed until years later. The two schools in Heeley itself are Heeley Bank, completed in 1880 and Gleadless Road School, later called Anns Road School and now Anns Grove. There were three sections, Infants, Girls and Boys. The subjects taught were reading, writing, arithmetic, English, history, geography, art, music and religious training. The girls were taught needlework and the boys geometry. Gleadless Road School, being built later than Heeley Bank, had more amenities for its scholars, including rooms for domestic science and metalwork. Students from Heeley Bank made use of these classes. Girls in the last year of school spent a day in a large house in Meersbrook Park Road for housewifery. The boys at Heeley Bank also worked in the school garden.

The Furniss Family of Heeley in about 1898. William Furniss, the son later ran a butcher's shop on corner of Gleadless Road/Florence Place.

In 1902 the government made another change in education, abolishing School Boards and transferring their duties to municipal authorities. This was the birth of Education Committees, and Heeley Bank and Gleadless Road schools became council schools. Higher education was being improved in the Sheffield area and Intermediate and Secondary Schools were opened. To gain a position in one of these schools the Scholarship examination had to be taken. This was in two parts, the first at one's own school. If successful, Heeley children went to Duchess Road School to take the second part. Successful students according to the position of their pass and the financial situation of the parents, then went to the school of their choice.

There were also private schools in the district, notably the Petch School attached to Heeley Wesley, which lasted into the present century. There was also Doctor Flory's School in Myrtle Springs which opened in 1831, and numerous Sunday Schools. All these Heeley schools have whole histories of their own.

Heeley Bank School
"My grandma Loy, who would have been over 120 years old now [born 1870s] was the eldest daughter of my Great Grandad and Grandma Hukin who moved to Thirlwell Road when she was few months old. Great Grandad had a horse and dray with which he used to deliver coal and also to collect and deliver balm (or yeast). The house in Thirlwell Road had stables and coach house for the horse and cart and this was the start of the yeast business that Hukins still run today. As a young child my grandma went to a school in Oak Street for two years but when Heeley Bank School was built and opened in 1880 she spent the rest of her school days there. She used to tell me how she had to climb up the hillside in the fields alongside the rhubarb fields once she got beyond the houses on Anns Road. The hillside had many springs and streams and in hot weather she used to paddle in the streams on her way to and from school. Of course Heeley Bank Road had not been built on then and the school was opposite the quarry on Cross Myrtle Road." **Barbara Lomas**

"We lived in Myrtle Road halfway between Anns Road and the top of Myrtle Road. Started school August 1895 at just 3 years. I can remember my mother taking me to school in the morning and fetching me back at dinner time, taking me back after dinner and fetching home for tea. Heeley Bank was the school. Miss May was the Infants Headmistress and Miss Cleghorn Headmistress over the Girls and Mr Snelgrove was Headmaster over the Boys. Schooling those days was confined mostly to three Rs reading, writing and (a)rithmetic. I think I left Heeley Bank when I was either 11 or 12 years old. I then went to Abbeydale School where the classes went on to standard 7 and +7. I was fortunate enough to get what was termed the Merit Certificate at Abbeydale. School life was not bad in those days, we went to the Public Baths once a week, Park Baths at first and then

when Heeley Baths were built on Broadfield Road we attended there. To the East and South of Heeley Bank School it was all fields and farms I remember Lawsons had a farm almost adjoining the school, the farm stretched over Black Bank right along to Abourthorne. He had several sons - one Tom who was in my class and I was good pals, hence I used to go to the farm quite a lot. He bad quite a good dairy herd and no milk marketing nor milk bottles. Milk was taken around in horse drawn milk float from door to door and sold at about 1¹/₂d a pint (old money). It was amusing to see the horses that pulled the float. He or she knew just where to stop and start without the milkman giving orders of command. Reverting back to school life, discipline was pretty severe, there was very little restrictions on caning. The class teacher and the Head all had a cane handy, or sometimes a strap, but mostly canes and according to the will of the Teacher the method of dealing it out was determined either six across the hand or touch your toes six times while he had a split second delivery of the cane. By Jove and didn't it hurt, and most of us made it worse by withdrawing the hand as the cane came down, consequently it landed on the fingers where it tingled worse, and more often than not if you complained at home or made too much of a song about it you got a second dose, so you kept quiet."
Charles Henry Stokes Born 25th August 1892

Later memories of Heeley Bank Infants School recalled by Joan Palfreyman.
"One morning for some reason my mother went on to school with me. It was raining heavily and when we got there a number of children were standing at the door which was locked. When my mother asked about this, we said that the key was inside the cloakroom window and one of the teachers had to unlock the door. She promptly opened the window, got the key and unlocked the door and let us in, then waited to see Miss Ludlam [the headmistress], when she arrived shortly afterwards, instead of a meek little group waiting in the rain, there was a gang of infants running up and down the corridor and in the cloakroom. Of course she was most indignant and wanted to know by whose authority mother had opened the door. Mother said she didn't need authority when the children were standing in the wet, a lot of them were poorly shod and clothed and it would mean them sitting in the wet until lunchtime and it was up to her [Miss Ludlam] to see that the door was opened. I don't know if she ever got around to what she had come to the school about, hut Miss Ludlam always seemed to have it in for me after that. Thinking about it nowadays, I don't think that she was ever the sort of person who should have taught young children, she was probably near retiring age and was keeping her head down until she could draw her pension.

I was about seven years old and had just realised what Armistice Day was all about. I knew that my uncle had been killed on the Somme and that my father had served in India and that the whole country stopped for two minutes at eleven in the morning. In those days we went to school in the morning and had a short service and had the afternoon holiday. We all stood for the two minutes silence, when it was over Miss Ludlam said that some of us had fidgeted [what did she expect of five year olds?] and we would have the silence again before we went on with the service. That utterly spoiled the whole thing for me, I thought what did it matter if you could alter things just to suit yourself? It was years before I really came to terms with it again.

The first hearing aid that I remember seeing was in the Infants School, it would be in the early nineteen thirties. The teacher who wore it was called Miss Shipman. It looked like a pink cork that fitted in her ear with a pink cord which presumably went down to a microphone. We always had to speak clearly in her class, she never called the register, but looked at us in turn and marked us off and then counted us to see if the numbers tallied. Sometimes she would ask us if such a person was there. Although my name is spelled Palfreyman it is pronounced Polfreyman, but Miss Shipman always pronounced it as Pal. I little thought that in fifty or so years time I would be wearing a hearing aid myself." **Joan Palfreyman.**

A former pupil of Heeley Bank School recalls the days she spent there just prior to and during the early years of the Second World War.
"Each morning my friend and I climbed the steep hill to the imposing edifice which stood at its summit, often reciting to one another poetry which we'd learnt by heart. I still remember the opening lines of one of Lord Macaulay's Lays of Ancient Rome – 'How Horatius Held the Bridge', which seemed to be one of my friend's favourites whilst I might recite his epic poem 'The Spanish Armada'. Morning lessons began with a daily dose

of spellings to learn from the blackboard, mental arithmetic including multiplication table and scripture which often consisted of learning passages from the Bible by heart. Copybook handwriting lessons were also frequent. Much of this was rote learning but it was nevertheless, to stand us in good stead in years to come.

I still remember some of the teachers who made such an impression on us for good or ill: Mr Sorby who read extracts from the novels of Robert Louis Stevenson to us on Friday afternoons, when the likes of 'Kidnapped' and the adventures of Jim Hawkins in 'Treasure Island' fired our imaginations. Who can forget the tall figure of Mr Goulding whom nearly everybody feared, Mr Whittlestone who introduced us to the mysteries of science or Mr Sisk (sadly later a prisoner of war in Japanese hands) who sat on a high stool, often teetering backwards as he taught? One day he leaned too far, fell over and landed on the floor to the amusement of all the class. Staff and pupils alike were presided over by the Headmaster, Mr Stockley, a Churchillian figure of vast proportions, who seemed constantly to be peering down on us from the window of his study which overlooked the central corridor, eagle eyes ever alert for any sign of incipient misbehaviour. Imagine our astonishment and disbelief when he married Miss Logan, the slim lady teacher who seemed almost young enough to be his daughter!

My friend and I often acted as monitors and were given various tasks and responsibilities. For a time one such responsibility which we didn't relish was to be in charge of the little son of our class teacher, (a lady who shall remain nameless), who came from nursery school for the last half hour of afternoon school. He was one of the naughtiest children we had the misfortune to meet! School bank money was collected every Monday morning and I was always apprehensive when sent with this to Mr Hill, the teacher in charge and a man of formidable reputation. He invariably asked my name and reminded me that he had taught my brother, ten years my senior. I always felt that this was an experience my brother would not have enjoyed.

Memories come flooding back of the opening years of the Second World War. The days of 'Home Service' when the school was closed, lessons rather erratically held in people's front rooms and girls' PE in the muddy farmyard at Ash Farm. School dinners were being introduced – watery vegetables and sago or 'frog spawn', as we called it, for sweet – lukewarm and coming in containers. Having sampled these we decided that we'd rather go home for dinner after all. 1942 arrived and we had reached the age to 'sit' the Scholarship. Neither my friend or I wanted to leave Heeley Bank, so no grammar school was chosen from the list on our application forms. For me the test meant nothing other than the possibility of a half day holiday after they were over. Imagine our astonishment, then, when our parents received letters from the Director of Education requesting our mothers to attend a meeting at the Education Offices on Leopold Street. At the meeting Dr Alexander, the Director of Education at the time, explained to the parents present that their children had passed the Scholarship high

Conkers in Heeley in the late 1930s

enough to merit a place in a grammar school. When asked if there were any questions my mother stood up and commented that she understood why boys should go on to further education for they would be breadwinners, but she expected her daughter to grow up, get married, raise a family and be a good wife and mother. Why should a grammar school education be necessary for her? I still feel some embarrassment when I think of this and yet my mother was only expressing the views current amongst many working class families of the time in contrast to attitudes in education today.

*Finally our parents were persuaded, reluctantly, to let us go to the nearest grammar school, which was a relatively new one, Hurlfield Grammar School for Girls, part of which was on Eastern Avenue on the Arbourthorne Estate. Thus my happy days at Heeley Bank School had come to an end." **Recorded by Betty Renshaw, herself a pupil of Heeley Bank School.***

The Gleadless Road/Anns Road/Anns Grove School

The foundation stone of a new school building was laid down in 1890 on a corner site of what was renamed Anns Road [formerly Quarry Lane or Mucky Lane] and the newly named Gleadless Road, the lower part of which had been called Sheaf Street. The preparation of the site included the tidying up of the old quarry and the demolition of three small cottages opposite the end of Wilson Place. One of the families which had to be rehoused was the Briddons. Local stonemasons were employed on the site to dress the stone blocks which had to be brought up the hillside by horse and cart from Heeley railway station where they had come by train from quarries at Grindleford. One of the masons was Mr. Akers who lived in a large house on Wellhead Road. The various school buildings and the sloping play grounds and the caretaker's house, the surrounding walls and locking iron gates were built and ready to admit pupils when the school was opened in January 1892.

There were separate schools and entrances for boys and girls and also for the different age ranges, so the Infant, Junior and Senior schools were all distinct with different staff and head teachers. The classrooms were large (60 or more children in each) and the floors were in large steps going up to the back of the room so that

Mavis Thornhill's brother Brian Fell in a back yard of Spencer Road.

the teacher could easily see all the children from the big desk at the front. Most of the children left the school at either thirteen or fourteen years of age, although some left at eleven if they passed the Scholarship Examination and went on to secondary [grammar] school, while the class six boys at Heeley Bank School were transferred to the Gleadless Road School for their final year's education.

*"The reception classroom at Gleadless Road School was always warm with its big fire and fireguard. I enjoyed riding on the big rocking horse. There was a small chair for each child and the tables were the right height for me to sit down and write, because I was always small for my age." **Olive Simpson.***

Over the succeeding years various changes occurred so that from time to time the youngest children were taught in mixed classes and on some occasions the infant and junior schools were merged under one head teacher but later separated again. Even the name of the school was changed - in the 1920s it was altered to Anns Road School, because after 1921 when Gleadless became part of Sheffield, mail for the Gleadless

Road school of that former village was being delivered to Heeley. Again in the 1980s the name was changed and it became Anns Grove School as the children from the Olive Grove area were transferred to the school following the closure of Heeley Bank school at the end of 1980/81.

Mary Barker, who remembers playing in her parents' allotments between Northcote Road and Cat Lane about 1950s.

Many personalities on the school staffs are well remembered by former pupils. Miss Edwards was a teacher of some of the first older girls to go to the school and she remained in charge of the eleven year old's scholarship class until her illness in 1940, when her place was taken by Miss Knight who continued to teach the eleven year olds until she retired in the late nineteen sixties. Many will remember Miss Prescott in the reception class of the girls infants and also Miss Hargreaves in the boys school who only died recently at the age of ninety six. The head teacher Miss Haird and her sister the "little" Miss Haird in the Junior School and Mr. Chandler and Mr. Hepworth on the boys staff are often referred to by old pupils. Mr. Bill Goulding is remembered as a strict martinet, whilst Mr. Wilson was a sports teacher who had a collection of canes from which a culprit could choose which was to be used to inflict punishment. Mr Davison is remembered as a woodwork teacher who taught at the night school as well as the day school and Mr Muxlow, a teacher at the senior boys school was unique in using a strap instead of a cane to punish pupils.

"I remember my first day at Anns Road School in the early 1930's. It was a cold January day but the reception class was welcoming with its fire surrounded by a huge fireguard. I was so excited because I had longed to start school ever since my older brother had started two years earlier. Miss Prescott who taught the reception class was so lovely that I felt at home at once. I was put a the beginners' table at the front of the classroom near the door, but when she discovered that I could already write my name and knew my alphabet she said, "I can see you will be moving up to the top table soon." I can remember that we all had a slate and chalk and a piece of old cloth – invaluable for us as tools to learn to write letters and numbers, do sums, learn to draw shapes and with a variety of coloured chalks, do pictures. I must have loved nature and trees and flowers even then because my favourite picture was to draw a few trees on a grassy bank with bluebell flowers and a path winding through it. Apart from the odd attempts at houses with chimneys producing lots of smoke I drew this kind of picture more than once. Even so I could draw lovely patterns with shapes and got good marks for them. I do not remember now what Miss Prescott looked like, but she was so kind, caring and loving towards the children that we all loved her and I'm sure she made the introduction to school enjoyable for so many children.

In the Junior School at Anns Road the teachers who taught me were Miss Johnson, Miss Schofield, Miss Wallace and Miss Edwards. Big Miss Haird was the headmistress, always referred to as 'big' because she was tall and slim in contrast to her sister, 'little' Miss Haird, since she was short and dumpy, but she never taught me. It always seemed to me that big Miss Haird was carrying the cares of the world on her shoulders – she rarely smiled and often frowned, but she always bent down with a kind look on her face whenever I was sent with a register or any other document to give her. Miss Schofield was young (or at least compared with the others, at that time all teachers were old to me) and I remember she had long hair worn in two plaits coiled over her ears. She became engaged while I was in her class and left when she got married. Miss Wallace was very prim and precise and I wrote a play about Guy Fawkes while I was in her class which we performed in the hall. My mother had been one of the early pupils when it was called Gleadless Road School (she started in 1895 aged 3) and Miss Edwards had taught her. Although she was strict and very stern in mental arithmetic and spelling lessons, I enjoyed being in her class. I remember we all took turns at shaking the cream collected from our milk at break in order to make butter when we were learning the work of a dairy farmer and his wife. I was fascinated by her geography lessons, especially on Canada, because she has spent a holiday there and her descriptions brought the place to life for me. I always enjoyed the Friday afternoon timetable which included some personal reading, a double art and craft lesson and at the end a lesson when she read a book to us. This introduced me to many classics besides those I had already discovered at the library myself. The sewing classes were amusing – I remember being taught how to make a pattern and when I was supposed to be making a pair of gym knickers I was asked if I wanted long or short legs on them. My reply was for short, but when the pattern was made up the legs came down to my knees, so my mother had to shorten them for me when I took them home. I still have the sewing apron that occupied most on one term, with various pockets, coloured trim and embroidered patterns by means of which we all learned how to sew using tacking stitches, hem stitch, back and fore stitch, running stitch and many embroidery stitches.

I took the Scholarship exam while in Miss Edwards' class and at the end of that year moved on to another school." **Lilian Haywood.**

Mary Barker's brother Jack remembers Anns Road School just before the war.

"In 1938 I started my education at Anns Road Infant and Junior School. which was only a short distance away at the bottom of Sturge Street. It was a typical old stone built school, with an asphalt playground surrounded by a high stone wall and a pair of large cast iron gates at the entrance.

Jack Barker's children in Sturge Street in 1966.

All the mothers would come down to the school gates at playtime to bring biscuits and drinks for their children, in winter they brought hot soup. The school gates were always closed during school hours to stop any young pupils from 'escaping'. We had a daily 'one third of a pint' bottle of milk complete with cardboard top and push-out hole where a drinking straw could be inserted. The milk was brought to the classroom by the 'milk monitor': a much sought after duty as it got you out of the classroom to carry up the crates of milk for your classmates.

My school days at Anns Road were very happy: all the teachers were excellent, my first teacher being Miss Hargreaves. I recall that other teachers were: Miss Lucas: Miss Wilson: Miss Humberstone: Miss Knight: Miss Jackson: and the Headmistress. Miss Haird. a very tall thin lady who had a sister also a teacher. another Miss Haird who was very small and dumpy. We used to call her 'Little Miss Haird' (But not to her face).

During this time (1940's) our school was closed and in its place, we had what was called, 'Home Service', when a group of pupils would use the front room of someone's house as a temporary classroom. I don't know whether or not I was lucky but my mother volunteered for our front room to be used at 83 Sturge Street. Boys and Girls were taught on alternate days, but, with me living there I got to attend all sessions .... Lucky old me, at least I could stay in bed longer and not have to go out in the cold to go to school! I was teased unmercifully by the boys, having to sit in with the girls. I wonder what they would think now! This form of education was to last for most of the war, but we did not seem to be any worse off, in fact with a more informal atmosphere it was quite often more fun than the conventional way of teaching. I am sure we learned far more this way."
Jack Barker.

The Petch School (Heeley Wesley Day School)
"The school was formally opened on January 10th 1870, Mr. W. Petch having been appointed Head Teacher and Mrs. Petch as Mistress. The fees were paid weekly in advance on Monday mornings, or on the first time in the week that the child had gone to school. From a recorded interview with Mrs. Webb, we learn that the school fee was 2d. per week. It is believed that if a pupil paid thirteen weeks in advance, one week's schooling was free. All the money collected from the pupils was kept by Mr. Petch, according to school Board rules, no assistant or pupil teachers were allowed to retain money collected as school fees. The courses of instruction included "Subjects of the Education code for the time", these being reading, writing and arithmetic. At the end of each school year, each pupil who had passed the inspector's examination in reading, writing and arithmetic received an illuminated certificate which stated the number of attendances male and the standard of examination passed.

Mr and Mrs Petch with a class of girls around the turn of the century.

The "Petch School" also taught other subjects, one of which being Biblical instruction.
The syllabus for the infants and the first three standards was:

Infants	- Learn the 10 Commandments, Exodus XX, the Lords Prayer and St. Mathew VI verses 9—13. Brief account of the early lives of Samuel and David. Leading facts in the life of Christ told in simple language.
Standard I	- Same as for infants - in fuller detail.
Standard 2	- Repeat the 10 Commandments and the Lords Prayer. Learn St. Mathew v.1—12 and Mathew XXII v.35—40. The life of Abraham. Simple outline of the life of Christ.
Standard 3	- Memory work as in standard 2. Learn St. John XIV v.15-31. The life of Moses. The life of Christ.

The school had to note the 14th section of the Education Act, which states that "no religious catechism or religious formulary, which is distinctive of any denomination", could be taught.

Singing was taught at the school along with physical exercises and drawing. Singing, prayer and scripture lessons were taken each morning by Mr. Petch. The school was closed in the afternoon in a similar manner by singing a hymn and by a prayer, again taken by the headmaster, Mr. Petch. Drill took place in the playground taken by a drill instructor who was helped by one of the teachers. The teacher was therefore learning the drills and eventually knowledgeable to teach drill. The school timetable provided for morning recreation in the playground, one teacher was in the playground in charge of the pupils.

The Petch School after 1902 came under the Sheffield Education Committee, whose regulations were slightly different to the school board rules.

Subjects of Instruction as stipulated by the Committee

a)	Biblical instruction
b)	Elementary instruction
c)	Geography and History
d)	Elementary science to children in Standards I) II) III) & IV).
e)	English to include hearing and speaking exercises, taking of notes and the use of a dictionary: composition and letter writing.
f)	Mechanics (for boys) Domestic economy (for girls).
g)	Needlework (for girls)
h)	Domestic subjects (for girls)
1)	Drawing
j)	Varied occupations
k)	Handicraft (for all boys of 11 years, where suitable centres are provided).
1)	Singing, by note, staff notation to be taught to scholars in Standards IV and upwards,
m)	Physical training
n)	Health and Temperance

The opening and closing times of the school were much the same, the only difference being the time which the infant school closed. After 1902 the infants finished at 4.00p.m., 20 minutes earlier than when the school came under the School Board. Sheffield Education Committee stipulated a maximum number of pupils allowed in each class at the Petch School, the number being 60."

Mr Petch was the great, great grandfather of Robert H Foreman who researched the above account.

Alun Montgomery has collected some tales about Mr Petch.
"Mr Petch was said to be a strict timekeeper. He lived on Albert Road and many of the local householders were said to set their clocks and watches to the right time as he walked past their houses on the way to school. Although most pupils acquired a sound education in the 3Rs, art, so dear to Mr Petch's heart, was expertly taught. Before the days of wax crayons the humble pencil was the main tool used to crate delicate dark and light shades. I remember visiting my old friend's house (his daughter was my music teacher) who attended Mr Petch's school at the turn of the century when I would stare in amazement at two pencil drawings on the wall. A lion, lioness and two cubs – I felt the lioness was poised to spring out at me at any moment. Secondly the interior of a blacksmith's workshop, complete in every detail, horses, anvil, furnace and many tools. Most boys in the school had artistic ability, sadly, however, a few were 'non-starters'. Mr Petch would select a

boy and tell him to draw a horse and cart for example. Mr Smith remembered the day when a non-starter was told to draw 'something' much to the amusement of the rest of the class. The poor victim hesitated, as if deep in thought, at last he set to work and drew a small circle on the board. A loud voice then thundered out, "Well boy, have you finished? What is it then?" A trembling reply followed. " A glassy, Mr Petch." To the uninitiated an explanation is required – a glassy is a marble!

In today's schools the teaching of punctuation is often ignored and children and adults make the same mistakes that an unfortunate boy made 100 years ago. A boy was told to punctuate the following sentence. 'The elephant said Charlie is the largest land animal.' After a few moments reflection he set to work and with a look of triumph on his face produced the following:-

'The elephant said, "Charlie is the largest land animal".' Mr Petch's reaction was instantaneous, "Very kind of the elephant to say that about Charlie!" Whether or not the unfortunate culprit emerged in one piece for the encounter I never knew." **Alun Montgomery.**

Heeley Friends

"In 1883 a school for teaching men to read and write was started in Heeley. A little later a school for women was formed and a children's Sunday School opened. Some of the older girls were housed over a cowshed in Gifford Road, where the warmth rising from the animals was welcome on cold days. These schools were developments from the Friends' First Day [i.e. Sunday] Schools which had been started earlier in the century by James Henry Barber, a leading Quaker, at Hartshead in Sheffield. The First Day Schools were regarded as both educational and a social service. The volunteers who ran the schools had also the idea of bringing working people to love and follow Christ, to understand the Bible, to apply Christian principles in all walks of life and to join in the fight against drunkenness, gambling and other unworthy forms of living. One of the early Heeley members, whose grand daughters still live in Woodseats, stopped drinking wholly out of respect for the men who gave time and effort to teach him. His wife, a member of the Women's School, provided the chair upon which speakers stood when open-air meetings were held outside the public house at the bottom of Gleadless Road. It was hoped that some members might be drawn to become Quakers. The Friends' First Day School movement was the result of efforts by Friends in many parts of the country, but there were also a number of groups run by non-conformist, church and other socially minded people that had similar aims and ideals. Eventually over many years, all were amalgamated into an independent, non-sectarian Adult School Movement.

The School at Heeley had the use of the Reading Room at Skelton's Sheaf Bank Works and a house in Prospect Road as well as the Gifford Road cow shed. Money raising efforts, e.g. selling "bricks", by the members and the generosity of Friends made it possible for a schoolroom to be built in Prospect Road. This was the home of Heeley Friends' First Day Schools, later, Heeley Adult School, known locally as "Heeley Friends". Though at various times Quaker meetings were held in the building, Adult School members became Quakers only if they applied to join the Society of Friends as anyone else might. Some were members of other denominations, but the majority belonged to none. At one time the rule was that the time of Adult School sessions should not clash with local church services so that members were free to attend their church and their school.

At the beginning, when reading and writing were taught, the Bible was the textbook and each member who became proficient was expected to teach someone else. "Each one teach one" was the rule. Later, the School sessions were based on Bible study and prepared topics for discussion literature, art, science, social studies and the like. In its heyday Heeley School had a Sunday morning men's class at one time over a hundred strong, a mid week women's class and a children's Sunday School run on Church Sunday School lines with around one hundred and fifty scholars. On Sunday afternoons men's women's and young people's groups opened together with hymns and prayers, separated for the "lesson" and closed together. Festivals such as Christmas were marked by special sessions, often taking the form of simple religious services, but the School was in no sense a church. This fact led to doubts about its eligibility to belong to the local Sunday School Union, but it was accepted in the end and played an active role in the Union, joining the "Whit Sings" in Meersbrook Park and other events. One member was MPSSU Secretary for some years and two conducted the hymns in Meersbrook Park.

Social, educational and religious facets of life were regarded as interlinked. During its lifetime the School ran a social club over a shop in Gleadless Road, a youth club, drama groups, concert parties, children's May Days with a May Queen, old folks' treats, outings, a rambling club, flourishing football and cricket clubs, bazaars, craft clubs, choirs and dances and produced several pantomimes which were initiated with the intention of getting old and young members to work together and get to know each other. A missionary group was formed in support of two members who went to Madagascar to teach in a Quaker School there. Al the work was done by volunteers. Officers and committee which kept the School running were elected by members, the whole organisation being organised democratically.

Heeley Friends Sunday School on May Day

Heeley School members played an active part in Adult school work in Sheffield, Yorkshire and nationally, helping to found a School at Woodseats and later groups meeting in home in other parts of the city.

Celebrations marking the School's 60th, 70th and 80th anniversaries were held. Soon after the latter a proposal to build a trunk road over the site threatened the School building. City development meant the demolition of local houses and people moved away from the area. Membership declined. The road was not, in the end, built, but the building was repeatedly vandalised. The children's Sunday School had to be closed and the few remaining adults continued to meet in member's homes. Eventually the building had to be demolished and the site is now a grassed over area. [The site is quite near the White Horse on the hillside between Prospect Road and View Road] Soon after the centenary in 1983 the last few members disbanded, most of them joining other Adult Schools in the city."

Grace Young

An illustration from 'Some of those Days - A Heeley Childhood'

Life

The first piece in this section is a contemporary account from a Sheffield newspaper from the 1870s, kept at Sheffield Local Studies Library. Copied out by Alun Montgomery.

"A few minutes sufficed to bring me down Sharrow Lane into the squalid region of Heeley. On passing Heeley Decorative and Art Company's premises, I derived an impression that decorations need not necessarily be artistic. From the Railway Station I reached Cambridge Road.

A new steep Street lined with red brick buildings, scarcely more than Cottages, where milk carts, coal carts, salt carts, rag and bone men and herring hawkers were busy going their rounds. (Sir Francis Chantrey as a boy went round with milk cans and Mr Steel of Steel, Peach. & Towzer admitted he once hawked herrings.) At the top of Cambridge Road I passed a chap seated in a donkey cart. "Haddocks, haddocks", He cried. He was beating his poor animal in a cruel fashion, which prompted an angry woman to put her head out of a window. "Eh mister, have you no mercy?" He replied with a vigorous jerk of the reins, "I've nought but haddocks".

Cottages on Heeley Green. *Sheffield Local Studies Library.*

Fifty years ago, Heeley was a village with a church and village green near Sheffield. It's hard to believe that the site was once occupied by a few old cottages and a long sheet of water. (River Sheaf) where teams bringing their loads to Sheffield would stop to drink. Near the bridge stood Heeley Tilt, this site is now occupied by Skelton's Works. Thick woodland extended to the bridge on Myrtle Road. All around were rich pasturelands and corn - fields."

The following account is from a recording of a conversation with Mrs. Nightingale and her husband, in their own spoken words of her life in the early 1900s. Her mother, Mrs. Styring, brought a cart round Heeley regularly.

"She was left, when she was 39, with seven children. My father died in the Nether Edge hospital, which you know was the workhouse. He had a sister that was Headteacher at Low Fields School when it first opened, and she said to mother, "you'll not sit with your feet on the fender, will you, love, you'll work hard for him?" So she went and bought some fish and she started with a basket from door to door, and she had such a good name. When she had been going a bit she said 'I think we will move out of Scarsdale Road, we'll go further down here, so we moved to Cliffefield Road.

When my father died, the insurance money, when we finished, there was half a crown left, and she bought a box of kippers with that I was five. I'm 83 now, so that makes it 1908. She sold the kippers, (and fish, which she bought at half-a-crown a stone). Then she decided to improve the business so she bought this donkey. She sold the kippers all round here (Norton and Norton Lees). She went on foot.

My mother had the donkey stabled up at the milk place in Beverley Road, then she sold him and my husband fetched the white pony for her. She had to have something a bit bigger because her fruit and vegetables business was increasing.

Of course from there, the business got a bit bigger, and she sold the donkey to the same man as she bought the pony off, on Saxon Road. It was a big pony, a white one. My husband went and fetched it and it took him all his time to hold it up Derbyshire Lane. It was like a little racehorse. And that was stabled at the same place up Beverley Hill, Mr. Shaws, milk people they were then. He used to fetch it corn and straw from Parker's, at the end of Broadfield Road, where they've pulled it down and built Heeley Bridge garage. Mr. Shaw used to feed it and bed it, sometimes my husband's gone and fed it and groomed it."

In the early 1890s, Harry Ponsford, a skilled silversmith in Sheffield lived with his growing family in a small terraced house in Myrtle Road, Heeley. Desperately needing to earn some extra money he collected payments in the evenings for the local coal merchant. He called in virtually every house both to take orders for coal and to collect monies due. During this time customers asked him to obtain household items and this was the start of the Ponsford shop.

The early days were a struggle, silver smithing by day and collecting most evenings, but it was by this enterprise that the family was able to move house, to a slightly larger dwelling each time. Trading from the back room changed to having a shop in Valley Road. It was by now the twenties and his son and daughter had grown old enough to help him. Colin, now aged 32, felt that the business would not grow further until it had a main road location. There he could sell the 1930s modern furniture that was such a dramatic change from the tastes of the twenties and before.

Number 581 London Road (still the registered office of the company) forms part of the shop today which now covers from 579-609 London Road with additional buildings stretching back to adjacent streets beyond. The building is steeped in the typical architectural detail of the late 19th century. Recently, considerable renovation work has been sympathetically carried out to restore the building.

Don Ross wrote many pieces for the Heeley History Workshop's early booklets.

"One summer night, I cannot remember the year, around 1923, we had a very bad storm. It lasted nearly all through the night, all the houses on the opposite side of Albert Road to us were flooded The river rose half-way up their passage ways, flooding the cellar kitchens to a depth of 5 feet. All the shops on Heeley Bottom were flooded, Wainwright's Drapers, Charles Ross's Factory, Heeley Coliseum Picture House, Deniffs Butcher's and Heeley Silver Rolling Mills.

A flood under Heeley Bridge, there have been frequent floods in Heeley throughout the years.
Sheffield Local Studies Library.

Broadfield Road "The Primrose" as we called it, was one big lake This was before the dairy was built.
The first coloured person I ever saw was in the middle 20s. A Jamaican boy scout stayed at my Grandma Longden's, he was here for a scout jamboree. My uncle was a scout, and so was I at that time. Stanley Jepson the famous Sheffield baritone who lived on Meersbrook Park Road was scout master at Anns Road Primitive, Methodist Church, now St Andrews Methodists, he had two West African scouts staying with him. I was in Norton Lees Scouts. The scout hut was in a field just past the church before the road was cut through to join

us with Derbyshire Lane. Just beyond our hut were some cottages approachable from Derbyshire Lane. Eventually a hut was built next to the Parish Hall, and even that has gone."

Jack Barker has recently been in contact with the group via e-mail and has sent us these memories of his childhood in Heeley.

"I was born in a small, 'two up & two down', terrace house at 83 Sturge Street, (since demolished) in Heeley, a suburb of Sheffield. Sturge Street was a cul-de-sac, with a small genel at the top giving access to Gleadless road. My parents were of working class, my father John, being a labourer at Edgar Allen steel works. My mother Edna, stayed home to do all the chores that housewives did in the days before the many labour saving devices we have now were even thought of. Living in the house with us were my Grandmother Elizabeth and Aunt Edith, so we were rather cramped for space, as were thousands of other working class people in the 1930's.

The houses in Sturge Street were of the terrace type, all the houses being linked together in one long continuous row with a communal yard at the rear divided by a low brick wall between every fourth house. Each block of four houses had an entrance passage from the street, which led to the back yard, two houses being on either side of the passage. All the houses had a very small garden at the back, most of them very well tended and full of colourful flowers. At the back of the gardens were a row of four, brick built, outside toilets, one for each house, in winter the cisterns would freeze solid. (No centrally heated bathrooms then!)

The houses were heated by an open coal fire in the downstairs rooms with occasionally, one in the bedroom, the coal being kept in a cellar under the house. The fireplace in the kitchen had a large, 'black leaded' and highly polished cast-iron oven alongside it in which most of the cooking was done. In one corner of the kitchen, which also served as the dining room, usually adjacent to the window, was a stone sink fitted with one cold water tap. A large open-topped copper boiler with a fire-grate underneath was positioned next to the sink. This was to heat the water for all the families' ablutions such as; washing clothes, pots, dishes, and also for baths.

Washday was a full day of hard work for mother. First the water had to be ladled into the copper and the fire underneath coaxed into life. After what seemed hours waiting for the water to boil, a zinc wash tub would be filled with the boiling water then the families' dirty clothes and soap powder were added. To agitate the washing a 'posher' was used, this was made of wood and in appearance was similar to a small five legged stool attached to the end of a stout wooden handle. This had to be pushed up and down and twisted around at the same time on the clothes in the tub. (This now being done automatically by the washing machine). The next operation was the 'rubbing-board', which was a horizontally corrugated zinc sheet enclosed in a wooden frame on which the clothes were placed and, after liberally coating with a bar of soap, had to be scrubbed up and down by hand in order to remove any stubborn dirt. The scrubbing action combined with the soap and hot water made the hands of anyone doing the washing very sore, but there was no other way to accomplish this task then. After washing, the clothes would be wrung out on a mangle, consisting of a large cast iron frame containing two heavy wooden rollers connected by cogs at one end to a large cast iron wheel with a wooden handle, to be turned by one hand, whilst feeding clothes through the rollers with the other. The clothes were then hung on a wooden drying rack, usually suspended from the ceiling by hooks with a pulley system that allowed the rack to be lowered for the clothes to be hung on, and then raised back up, out of the way of the occupants in the room. Having a bath was a similar time consuming operation. The water having to be heated in the copper boiler, and then, a large zinc bath reminiscent of the bottom half of a coffin, would be brought up from the cellar (where they were usually stored) and placed in the 'front room' on the hearth in front of the open fire. The hot water was then transferred to the bath by using buckets. (How times have changed!)"

Letters are often sent to the group in response to an article or simply because the writer has heard we are interested in anything to do with Heeley.

"Everyone in Heeley will remember Taggy's ice cream, but what about the other old ice cream seller, Barkers of Gregory Road? They had a house window shop as well as a corner general shop. They made their own ice cream and had one of the old-fashioned handcarts which had a drum of ice all round the inner drum of ice cream. Mr. Barker used to get some local lads to push the cart to a pitch at the end of Carrfield Street and his son,

who was a cripple, stood and sold the ice cream. It was a race to get that pitch, because it was a regular meeting place along with Jack Allen's drink shop which was a few doors away. Mr. Barker's son was also a very good pianist and he played a large grand piano in the very posh lounge of the Red Lion public house on Heeley Bottom. Mr. Thomson was the landlord and very strict he was, you were not allowed in that lounge unless you had a collar and tie on! The Red Lion was one of our meeting places when we

The corner of Heeley Green and Alexandra Road
Sheffield Local Studies Library.

went dancing at Meersbrook Vestry Hall on Saturday nights. It was a great night out with a five piece band called the Cavendish all for a bob [1/- in those days]. Talking about dancing, when one of my brothers and I learned to dance we went to the Guild Room over the Co-op. in Gleadless Road every Friday night) price fourpence. You had to get past the caretaker who sat at the door. If he didn't like you he tried to stop you going in, so we had to go in with our parents who also attended. That caretaker was Mr. Neil, a small very bowlegged man, who sat for hours on end on his front window sill which was almost built for him. It was the second house at the beginning of Richards Road. Next door lived Little Dick who owned the coal shed next to Heeley Green, where you could buy half a hundredweight of coal and borrow one of his barrows to take it home. The shed is still there and it is now used by a joiner. Just another item of interest, my first job which I did at twelve years of age was to work at weekends at Broadhead's beer—off shop at the corner of Gleadless Road and

Gleadless Road looking towards the Victoria. The corner of Carrfield Road is on the left.

Carrfield Street. I worked from 5 o'clock to 9 o'clock on Friday night and on Saturday from 8.30 in the morning until 9 o'clock at night, taking orders out and weighing up flour and sugar into bags. My wage for all that was 2/6 and a bottle of pop. Still it was good grounding and I don't regret it." **B.Humphreys [late of Romney Road]**

"On childhood recollection, didn't our parents and grandparents work hard, black-leading the Yorkshire range, even before lighting the fire in the morning. I remember, my Mother black-leading our range with a brush, then, polishing it and finally polishing with a piece of old velvet type material cloth, then out came the emery paper for the shiny steel parts. These all had to be worked on until the result was bright and shining. But the bread and oven-bottom cakes were beautiful that came out of it so perhaps it was all worth the work.

All the floors had to be scrubbed and polished on one's knees. Then washing day, when the fire was put under the copper ready to boil water to put the washing in. I've seen my Mam scrub my Father's butchers overalls and aprons until veins stood out on her hands. There were no bathrooms. We used to have a tin bath in the front of the fire for which the water used to all have to be boiled first.

Every Spring cleaning time Mam used to put clean sheets on the floor of our attic and open all the pillow cases and bolsters and carefully empty the feathers out in separate piles to wash the pillow cases. Then after washing the cases and ironing them with a flat iron (no electric ones), we had the task of putting the feathers back, then sewing them up again. My Mam got her labour-saving goods later on but she certainly worked hard when I was growing up." **Mrs. Marie Gregory**

Church hall and Sunday School rooms were often used for special occasions. They were often the scenes of special concerts or bazaars to raise funds to maintain the buildings and pay for heating and lighting. Dorothy Ward, who lived in Albert Road as a girl, and married Clifford Mills the tenor singer, often performed monologues in dialect at such events. In the early 1900s the Heeley Balaliaika band used to hire a room at the Red Lion in which to practice. Grace Young's father and his sister used to play in this band in their teens and early twenties. Mr and Mrs Bagshaw remember having their wedding reception in the Salvation Army building (which was then the old Sheaf Street, on Gleadless Road) well over sixty years ago.

"I remember attending the wedding in Heeley Church of Jessie Weaver to Alfred Quincy in the early part of the war, the 1940s. The reception was held in the school room behind the vicarage so we only had a short walk from the church to the reception. Apart from the meal and some dancing my most vivid memory is of the bride sitting down to play the piano and her new husband standing beside her to sing 'Trees'. She taught young children to play the piano and Alf had a strong baritone voice, and I thought it was all very romantic." **Lilian Haywood.**

There were not many other venues large enough for many people to party, but wedding receptions and coming of age parties were sometimes held in the Guild Room above the Co-op.

"My brother, Eric Boot and his fiancée Margaret Warburton, booked the Guild Room of the Sheffield and Ecclesall Co-op in Heeley to have their wedding reception." **Joyce Jenkinson.**

"My cousin had her 21st birthday party there and a neighbour's daughter booked her wedding reception there in the 70s." **Lilian Haywood.**

"My father, Frank Badger, became caretaker and Boiler Fireman at C.T. Skelton in 1945, after he was demobbed from the army. My mother, Constance, worked in the firm during the day and cleaned the offices in the evening. My brother, Peter and myself earned our pocket money by giving Mum a hand with the sweeping, mopping and dusting. The works yard and all the different process work departments around it became our big adventure playground when all the workers had gone home. When I married in 1954, the

guest list eventually outgrew the size of the venue that my parents had booked and they were in desperate search for somewhere bigger. It was someone's bright idea to use the works canteen at C.T. Skelton. An unusual sight it must have been with bride, bridesmaids and all the guests dressed up in their best, trotting across the works yard and up the concrete steps or queuing for the goods lift. Still the marriage endures, unlike C.T. Skelton."
Sylvia Wright, nee Badger.

Jack Barker recalled the beginning of the Second World War and the Sheffield Blitz.
"11.15a.m. September 3rd. 1939, I was playing in our back yard with my next door neighbour Eric Sharman, when we heard the famous broadcast of the then Prime Minister Neville Chamberlain. He said, "I issued an ultimatum that unless satisfactory assurances of German action to call off the attack on Poland are received by 11am a state of war would exist between Britain and Germany. No such assurances having been received we are now at war with Germany." We of course, could not realise the implications of this, and our excitement was great, but this soon wore off as rationing; blackout; and all the other wartime restrictions were imposed.

Sylvia Wright (nee Badger) and husband at their wedding reception in Skelton's canteen

During the war (1939 1945) our school was used, like many others, as an Air-raid warden post, where all the residents in the area went to be issued with gas masks and taught how to use them. This included going into a wooden hut where we had to put on our gas masks, then gas was introduced from a canister. After a while we were told to lift a corner of our gas mask to smell what the gas was like in order that we would be able to recognise it. There were many different types of gas mask. For babies the mask was more of a canvas holdall that fully enclosed the baby. A small window was at the front enabling the mother to see the face of the child. Air was filtered and forced into the 'holdall' by means of a bellows type hand pump. For Toddlers the mask had a pair of ears fitted and the eyepieces were larger than the standard types. These were called 'Mickey Mouse' gas masks and were coloured, in the hope that they would not frighten the children.

The adult version was just plain black rubber with a canister containing a filter dangling in front. They were most uncomfortable to wear as they had to form an air tight seal against the wearer's face, being adjusted by canvas straps round the back of the head. There was a comic element about them in as much that when you breathed out it made a noise. (Like someone blowing a 'raspberry')
Sheffield was a prime target for German aircraft to bomb due to it being a major steel producing City manufacturing gun barrels along with shells and bombs.

I lived through the horror of the blitz on the night of 12/13th December 1940 when German aircraft from the Cambrai south airfield in France came over in three waves. The first wave consisted of 36 JUNKERS-88s and 42 HEINKEL-III bombers; the second wave, 23 JU-88s; 74 HE-IIIs and 7 DORNIER-17 bombers; the third wave, 63 JU-88s and 35, HE-IIIs, 280 bombers in all. For what seemed like hours we heard the distinctive drone of the bombers engines ... , the swish and scream of the bombs as they plummeted to their

targets followed by the almighty explosions, the ground shaking violently like an earthquake, intermingled with the sounds of anti-aircraft guns being fired.

In the morning a great pall of smoke hung over the City, tram-cars gutted by fire blocked the streets, and where once had stood buildings, nothing but piles of smoking rubble with the awful stench of burning and choking dust. Many hundreds of people had lost their lives this night but it was to be repeated yet again two days later on the night of 15/16th December when 66 HE-III and 11 DO-17 bombers came over to finish off what the main force had missed before. I had just undergone my baptism of fire but many more such nights would have to be endured before the war ended." **Jack Barker**

Percy and Elsie Wright at the back of 130 Myrtle Road in early 1920s

The war evokes many strong memories in our members and friends.

"The picture of Thirlwell Road in an issue of 'Old Heeley' brought back memories of my aunt and uncle, Ted and Edith Morgan who, as newly weds, lived at the top of the road in the 1930's. Sadly, their home was hit by a landmine during the Blitz. They were unharmed, thanks to an air raid shelter, but their neighbours – a family I think by the name of Wanless, were all killed.
I remember my father helping my uncle to salvage anything they could from the wreckage. One evening they found the top of a china cabinet and as light was fading had to leave it until next morning, in the hope that looters wouldn't get there first. They were lucky. To everyone's utter amazement, when it was unearthed, every piece of china was completely intact." **S Stanley**

On VE Day Evelyn and Winnie Wright, who lived on Myrtle Road, heard that there was a crowd of people gathering on Queens Road, near the Earl of Arundel pub. So they hurried down to join the fun. Someone brought a piano out of one of the nearby houses and there was singing and dancing in the street.

VE Day looking down Sturge Street. Jack Barker on front row, right.

Living in Heeley was like living in a large village where neighbours were not only friends but were also related. It was not uncommon to find grandparents, married sons and daughters and their children living in adjacent streets or 'just round the corner' or even in the next yard.

A real sense of neighbourliness developed in the mini-communities, so that if an elderly widow who lived alone was not well a neighbour would take in some hot broth for her at midday, or would bake her a couple of bread cakes in her own batch of baking. During a mother's confinement neighbours would help look after her older children and see she had all she needed until her husband came home from work. Even if a married son or daughter lived further away they would frequently visit their parents and would come back to the family church where they were married to have their children baptised, as can be seen by looking at the church or chapel registers.

Prospect Terrace, just off Prospect Road in the 1960s. Sheffield Local Studies Library.

"Living in Prospect Terrace as a child was like living in a large extended family, it was all so friendly and everyone helped anyone in need. My grandma and aunts lived 'round the corner' and all the children played together." Mavis Thornhill.

"When I was a child I spent a lot of time at my (maternal) grandparents and although we moved house several times it was always in Heeley and not far away from where we lived before. When I and my sister got married we continued to live in Heeley, near where we had been born and brought up." Eddie Chapman. [Mr Chapman has lived in Heeley all his life, 99 years in January 2001, and has lived in at least sixteen different houses.]

Before 1914 there were some areas of Heeley where many people were on the breadline and children had to stay away from school for lack of shoes. There was often no money to pay a doctor. Once when Mr Chapman's grandparents were ill, *"She couldn't pay the bill. In settling the bill Dr Fordham took her most treasured possession, an etching on copper of the Battle of Trafalgar. That was what happened – they had to give what they had."*

Mavis Thornhill's grandma and aunt watching over a toddler on Prospect Terrace.

The worst health hazard to the cutlers was the sand and dust from abrasive and polishing powders used in the trade. It effected their lungs and coughing was general, persistent and tiring. Dr McCallum, whose surgery was in Spencer Road, recalled the grinder's disease prevalent between the wars. Sometimes he put men off work suffering from exhaustion. Being 'thrown on t'panel' ie being off work with a doctors note, one could claim a small weekly state payment. To supplement this the local 'Sick and Divide' clubs to which members contributed 3d or 6d a week paid out small sums in times of sickness and death, any surplus money being divided between members at the year end. Overwork shortened some doctor's lives too. In the flu epidemic of 1957 Dr McCallum had to work alone. *"Besides the routine visits I had five hundred cases of flu between Monday and Friday. They were living around the surgery. It would be open from eight in the morning to midnight."*

Dr McCallum found Heeley people hardy, self reliant and neighbourly. Mr Chapman's grandmother lived on Heeley Green. *"She lived in a big yard and there was eight or nine houses and if anybody was sick there was always someone to there to fetch the doctor or to look after them and if someone was really poor someone would say, 'I've got so-and-so left. Would you like it?' They would make an excuse to help them and they did help each other at birth or death."* **Eddie Chapman**

Arthur Richards collected rents from houses in the Prospect Road area. He recalled that when visiting the houses on this picture the one at the end was on so much of a slope that a tea cup put on the table could not be filled up to the top.

Skelton's chimney is in the background and the river is sandwiched between the houses and the railway lines. Before the railway was built this area would have overlooked the Heeley Tilt Mill pond (see page 10). It is now a motor repair workshop and car sales business.

The houses at the bottom of Prospect Square off Prospect Road overhung the river.
Sheffield Local Studies Library.

"I was very shy at school, but I made friends with other children living in neighbouring houses in Sturge Street. We used to play games together like ball games, marbles and hopscotch using the flagstones on the pavement. Skipping was an activity that could be played alone or with others. With a long enough rope and two big girls to turn it several children could skip together and run in and out of the line singing skipping rhymes. One rhyme went 'House to let, apply within, when Mary goes out, Susan goes in' and you changed the names to suit the players. I'm not sure how to spell this one but it went 'Ala Bala Busha, king of the Jews, bought his wife a pair of shoes, when the shoes began to wear, Ala Bala Busha began to swear.' I haven't a clue who 'Ala Bala Busha' was! At other times we'd play whip and top, putting a drawing pin in the middle of the top and drawing chalk patterns round it." Mary Barker

"I was born in Gregory Road in 1942 and attended Anns Road School. One of my earliest memories was standing in Well Road watching the firemen damping down after the fire at Oak Street Chapel & my school teacher coming to take me back into school. I can still remember a lot of the shops which I used to pass on my way to school. Amy Morton at the corner of Forster Road & Boyton Street who used to accept soap powder coupons in payment for sweets, the Off Licence on the other corner, Heeley's Chemist shop, Hudson's Newsagents (later Staley's) Mrs Moss Ladies Fashions, Mrs Hunter Fancy Goods and Glassware and on the other side of Forster Road at the corner of Gleadless Road, Gowers. Just up Gleadless Road from Gowers was Stan Carter the barber. The last house on Forster Road before the shops was the Doctors who later moved to Kent Road." Dr. J. P. Thompson.

On Sunday morning's my father always used to take me to see his Mother & Sister who lived in Sturge Street. My Aunt Emmie, was for many years manageress of the wool shop on Heeley Bottom, Vickers. Mr Colley, the Newsagent in Gregory Road, was our landlord. My father's nickname for him was "Snow White" because he never looked clean. I used to go to Kent Road Sunday School and transferred to St Andrews when I joined the Life Boys there. I later became Sunday School Captain and the May Queen was Kathleen Booth. This was two years before Linda Guthrie and John Bunting whose picture was in a previous issue of Old Heeley. [See picture on page 37 on this book.]

My Mother's mother lived in Kent Road at the back of the Waggon and Horses Public House. The houses had cellar kitchens, which made ideal playrooms when it was wet & the large back yard was excellent for football & cricket. I also remember the Chip Shop in Boyton Street owned by Mrs Scales and her son Ken. This was a frequent haunt on my way home from courting. (They were usually open until about 1.00am.) I moved out

of Heeley in 1969 when I got married. I have many happy memories and still come back on a regular basis. Back to my roots." RH Deakin

Kent Road, behind the Waggon and Horses. *Sheffield Local Studies Library.*

Sport and Leisure

A Cautionary Tale To Sunday School Scholars. Extract from Heeley Parish Magazine 1901.
"The other Sunday one of our Sunday School scholars, on going home, passed a party of lads playing at "pitch and toss" The detectives pounced on the party, with the result that our scholar was served with a summons, to the great trouble of the lad and his father, who came to me. I went to the Police Station with the lad's attendance "Star" Card, which showed he had never once missed his class all the year. Moreover, he always brings his Bible, and contributes to the Missionary box. Happily, there was no proof of his playing and I believe the lad to be quite innocent. At my intervention the Chief Constable kindly withdrew the summons. My reason for naming this is to warn our boys on leaving the Sunday School to keep as far away as possible from the gangs of thoughtless lads who play at pitch and toss, or they may be taken for one of them, and fall Into the hands of the police."

Before the First World War and up to the coming of motor transport children were not afraid to play in the streets. In Heeley the coarse rope from greengrocery boxes was in demand for skipping. Spinning tops, marbles and shuttlecocks each had their season, and ball games, tiggy and hidey were popular.

A short walk up Gleadless Road brought you to the fields above 'T'Cuckoo' (Inn) each of which had its name and character; the daisy field, the buttercup field, the hillocky fields and so on. In some of these one could play and go sledging in the winter. Some were very steep. Twice a year the children from the Infant School were taken for a walk as far as an old grassed-over mine (quarry?) higher up Gleadless Road. Children used to go there on their own. *"Baby would be in the push chair with a bottle of cold tea and some bread and dripping. They were good days. We used to go there and nobody would bother. We walked for miles. We walked to Gleadless and over to Graves Park."* Graves Park was a private park then, but it was opened in winter for skating on the lake. On the way to Graves Park, in Norton Lees Lane, was a cottage where children could buy home-made ginger beer, and another up Gleadless Road where lemonade was sold. Ice cream, made locally by Taggy's was popular.

Children played in the old Northcote brick works known as the 'Docker'. *"'Bobby' Blower, he had a garden at the bottom and he was like the caretaker, and when he saw us playing in it he used to come and chase us out. Now we think about it probably for our own safety, I mean, because it was derelict. It was all shale from the quarries and brick yard that got piled that way and that way. And to make a road, which is Carrfield Road they made a cutting and that's how it got its name of 'Cutting'. We never went down Carrfield Road, we always went down the Cutting. Well, it were different to what it is now, obviously. They must have excavated it, and on the other side it was all rough clay in parts and we had football pitches on, didn't we? and cricket pitches"* Later a jam factory was built there (Geldart's), later Hydes and Spears.

The origin of the name 'Docker' for the area around Carrfield Road has been heavily debated in the Heeley History Workshop. Eventually this explanation was put forward.
"The name Docker came about because of the way in which the men who worked there were treated by their employers. At the Northcote end of the Docker, before ever the Cutting was made, there used to be a quarry and some of the men working in it were given the job of quarrying slates for roofs, these would be the old fashioned stone slates which were used on cottage roofs. Each day they were given a certain stretch of the quarry to work, for which they were to be given an agreed amount in payment. However, when pay day came , if they hadn't completed their stretches, their pay was docked – so much was deducted from the agreed amount. The employers were crafty, since it was a difficult job to get slate of the right size and they always made the stretch to be worked bigger than the men could finish in the time available. In this way they were always able to dock the wages. Eventually the men realised this and always referred to it as 'Goin' to work on t'docker'." HHW

"A couple of hundred yards past the [Heeley Bank] school up Myrtle Road was the Ball Inn Public House which had a large sports ground adjoining the Public house, this ground was entirely surrounded by a high stone wall. The ground was used at the weekend by local football clubs and cricket teams also during the summer evenings you could see the Bookmakers on the way up to the ground to take bets on handicap races. Crowds of people

used to attend these races and I surmised a good few lost their wages. Pigeon shooting was also a very popular weekday afternoon sport. Dozens of live birds were taken to the ground in baskets and let loose. Some were lucky and others not so lucky. It was quite a regular occurrence for a dead pigeon to fall in the school yard. There was a big rhubarb field between the school and the sports field and anybody who liked pigeon pie and had a dog with a good nose could mostly find an odd bird or two after the shooting was over and be sure of a meal. Mr Lawson the farmer let off two of his fields for cricket and football, one to Heeley Friends, one to Oak Street Chapel, games were played on a Saturday afternoon and the rivalry between local clubs was pretty lively. The country side in those days was very open and pleasant you could walk from just past the Ball Inn through Back Woods right to Gleadless and hardly see a house or branch off over Arbourthorne to Intake. On the brow of the hill near Arborthorne was a fairly large pond, where in winter a few went skating. Half a mile or so after leaving the Ball Inn and branching right you come across Gleadless Road and have a delightful walk through Rollinson Wood to Bagshaw Arms and Chantry land or come through what was called the Plantation past Clarks farm and through Lees Hall Golf Course, alas all this lovely country is gone now and crowded with houses, I suppose the extension of a city is inevitable but at what a cost." **Charles Henry Stokes**

Despite the presence of so many hills in Heeley, it is surprising how many local people found flat spaces to play their football. Part of the land on which Low-fields School now stands [it was built in 1873] was the ground for the old Heeley Football Club, in the days of its infancy and before it acquired a higher reputation, The players used a room in the Earl of Arundel and Surrey as a changing room. Eventually the club used a pitch in Meersbrook Park for their home matches.

Many people do not realise that Heeley was the original home of the famous Sheffield Wednesday Football Club. It was started at the Olive Grove ground in 1866 with amateur players who were mostly local lads and they didn't play professionally until 1887. The Sheffield United football ground was developed on Bramall's fields and the lane alongside those fields was made into the road which became Bramall Lane. Playing there was also amateur, since professional football was accepted at Bramall Lane in 1885. Sheffield United used the ground at the Ball Inn as their practice ground until the last couple of years. No wonder there was such fierce competition in Heeley between the Wednesdayites and the Unitedites.

In addition to these now-famous teams there were many amateur sides in Heeley. All the Heeley Churches, Chapels and Sunday Schools had their teams and played regularly in local league matches, e.g. the Sunday School League and the Bible Class League and so on. Other teams and leagues were involved with pubs or clubs or even local areas, as with the 'Cambridge Villa' team which was formed by keen lads who all lived in Cambridge Road. Mr. Fish had a sports shop on Heeley Bottom and ran a football league for sixteen-year-olds. The fields on which they played were rented from local farmers and they were often quite a distance away from the home base. Since the fields were used by the farmers for grazing during the week, the goalposts had to be taken there and erected for each match. The Heeley Friends team played on Black Bank and Kent Road Mission Team played on a field beyond Cat Lane and Lees Hall near the Lees Hall Golf Club. Valley Road also had a field up there, where Newfield School now stands.

Anns Road PM Chapel Football team. Harry Bussey back row 2nd from left.

The local schools also had junior football teams which competed in School League matches. The boys were fiercely competitive and gave their teams or opponents nicknames as when the [G]Nats played the [F]Lees - meaning the teams from Heeley National School in Gleadless Road and Norton Lees School on Kent Road [now called Carfield School on Argyle Close]. We know that Heeley Bank School formed their football club in 1884 at the time when the other main schools in Heeley were the Heeley National and the Petch Day School at Heeley Wesley.

The Hunt used to meet at the Newfield Inn on Denmark Road and there was always a good turnout to see them because many of the local residents acted as dogwalkers for the young hounds of the pack. Sightings of foxes around the Cat Lane Woods and allotments are quite common even today, so in the past we assume that they would not have had any difficulty in putting up a fox for the hunt.

Above: Spear and Jackson Team Photo. Harry Bussey on front row 2nd from left.

Right: Harry Bussey being carried off while playing for Scarborough football team. He never played again as a professional

It is a well recorded fact that there were trout in the Meers Brook before the tannery was established on Valley Road which polluted the water. So whereas today the water of the brook yields only very small limpets, water slaters, leeches and bloodworms with fresh-water shrimps in the upper reaches, the art of trout tickling would be familiar to some Heeley folk a hundred or more years ago. Even so, the anglers of Heeley would travel further afield for their pleasure - many of them taking a half day or day trip from Heeley Station on special excursion trains. Later, with the introduction of charabancs, angling clubs would book one for a day's fishing match. There were many fishing clubs in Heeley, nearly all the Churches, Chapels and Sunday Schools and most of the local Public Houses running their own clubs. Many of their outings and matches were arranged in Nottinghamshire and Lincolnshire, very popular areas including Retford, Boston, Wisbech, Ely, Worksop and Gainsborough or Killamarsh. Locally they would walk to Ford Bottom for a day's fishing and a picnic. Heeley St. Peter's had a fishing club and lads from Anns Road, Oak Street Heeley Friends and Brunswick Trinity joined together and made up a team who used Jack Allen's, herbalist shop on Gleadless Road as a base for their organised outings and matches. Heeley St. Peter's cup is still in existence with Mr Gear who won it in the last year that the fishing match was held. Mr. Chapman remembers one year in which his father, elder brother and himself won the first, second and third places in the annual match. As they were going to their pitches Mr. Chapman was given some bait by an old angler who was packing up and had had a good catch it was some partly cooked pearl barley and the fish had obviously found it palatable. Mr. Chapman's father used it and had bigger catches than anyone else using traditional bait, he used a double hook and managed to catch two fish at a time. Shooting was also organised in clubs, which were mainly based in the pubs. Some local people would also go out on their own or in twos, to the local woods, but if they were going down Cat Lane they had to be careful since one of the residents at Rose Cottages near the bridge over the Meers Brook was the gamekeeper for Rollestone Wood and Herdings. Wood pigeons and rabbits were commonly shot but perhaps the odd grouse or partridge would sometimes find its way into a Heeley cooking pot. We know that the Newfield Inn on Denmark Road had a very active gun club with yearly competitions, but we do not know where these contests took place, perhaps some of our readers could tell us.

The Gun Club outside the Newfield Inn on Denmark Road. The Landlord at the time was Mr Pemberton

The playing of bowls has been a game for Heeley ladies and gentlemen for a very long time. The old stagecoaching inn, the Red Lion on London Road had a bowling green on the flat land behind it before the ground rose to Thirlwell Road.

The bowling club on Shirebrook Road was formed when the road was developed in the eighteen fifty's. At that time the road was called Victoria Road and the gentlemen's' houses erected on it formed part of the Shirebrook Land Society. When Meersbrook Park was bought by the council in 1887 for Sheffield citizens, two bowling greens were established near the tennis courts, which are still in use today. The Meersbrook Park bowling teams for gentlemen, ladies and mixed teams have had a very long and successful history, with many Heeley residents playing a leading part in that success.

With all the steep hills in Heeley, you would have thought that none of the local people would have had contact with the game of golf, apart from the fact that most of them would not have been able to afford what has always been thought of as a rich man's hobby. However, the local people would often go for walks along Cat Lane and near Lees Hall and the woods, so they had a 'back door' entrance to the lower end of the Lees Hall golf course and became familiar with the 'plus fours' and other gear of the golfers and the familiar cry of "fore" before they teed off.

In fine weather, many Heeley children played their own game of golf - using inverted walking sticks as clubs and whatever small balls were available to them, sometimes even real golf balls. Some of these games were played in backyards or courtyards, but in summer they were also played in the daisy field and the hillocky fields near the Cuckoo[The Prospect View]. Over the years many Heeley children, especially the boys, went searching round the edges and the rough of the golf course for lost balls. Any that were found were sold back to the golfers who had lost them and so many a Heeley lad earned his weekly pocket

Heeley Electric Palace later known as Heeley Picture Palace.
Sheffield Local Studies Library.

money! Some of the local lads went even further than this and took up caddying at Lees Hall for the players. Among the caddies were two Tanfield brothers who lived in Penns Road, Alfred Smith and his brother who lived on Northcote Road and two of the Lees brothers who lived in the terrace at the Cuckoo. From caddying, several of them went on to learn to play the game on the Lees Hall golf course.

Heeley Electric Palace was built by George Longden and Son Ltd. It was opened on August Bank Holiday, August 7th 1911. It was first closed on March 6th 1963 and became a Star Bingo Hall. Films were reintroduced on February 28th 1965 as a dual entertainment with bingo and finally closed as a cinema on June 22nd 1965 to return to bingo. For a short period it was used as a skateboard rink and then as a furniture warehouse. There was a fire and it was finally demolished in 1981. The site is now a car showroom.

Heeley Coliseum was opened to the public on October 28th 1913. The cinema was reconstructed by Longden sometime before 1935. It was closed on January 14th 1961 and later demolished. A super market was built on the site and is now a plant and machinery depot.

A programme from Heeley Picture Palace. Films advertised this week include 'The Quiet Man' with John Wayne and Walt Disney's 'Pinocchio'.

Heeley Green Picture House was built by M.J. Gleeson Ltd. and was opened on Easter Monday April 5th 1920. It showed silent films in black and white. Mr Chapman remembers seeing Will Rodgers, a knockabout comedian, in a film in which he becomes involved in a cross country foot race by accident that he eventually wins.

In 1930 it became a variety theatre. There was a change of production each week and Mr. Chapman's sister, Mrs. Gandy, remembers that her husband was involved in dismantling scenery after the last performance on Saturday night and getting it down to the railway station ready for transport for their next venue for Monday. He usually had to walk back home and often it was after 3.30 am when he got in. His pay was half a crown. At Christmas time about five different pantomimes were shown, each being given for one week. The animals being used on stage in the pantos or other productions were kept in the back yard of the Waggon and Horses public house opposite the theatre. The members of the casts of the plays and pantos used to lodge for the week in nearby houses, in Denmark Road, the Newfield Inn, some in Romney Road and some in large houses down on Meersbrook Road.

Heeley Coliseum on London Road.
Sheffield Star.

Heeley Green Cinema as a Bingo Hall
Sheffield Local Studies Library.

It reverted to a cinema on May 9th 1938. *"Saturday evenings were great round about Heeley Green Cinema. There were two performances then and at the end of the first performance, what with the first house coming out and others hurrying to join the queue for the second house it was a busy as Piccadilly Circus."* *"I remember during the war, when it was a cinema my brother was home on leave from the army. He offered to take me to the pictures as a treat and after checking what was on elsewhere, we went to the Heeley Green cinema to see Laurence Olivier in Henry Vth."*

It closed on March 7th 1959 and was reopened on April 3rd 1961. The final closure as a cinema was on June 3rd 1962. There was talk of it becoming a Civic Theatre but this fell through. It was opened as a bingo hall and for a time was very popular, a special "bingo bus" being run free on to the Gleadless Valley Estate each night. When bingo went down in popularity it was converted to "Potters' Snooker Club".

Shops

In the first half of the twentieth century it used to be said that you didn't need to go into Sheffield to buy anything – whatever you needed, either food for your family, clothing from head to toe, or household goods, it was all available from Heeley Traders and business men and women from their shops or premises. Even with the introduction of radio (and later television) Beardow's shop in Gleadless Road provided all you needed, and offered a recharging service for your batteries. He later moved to larger premises on Heeley bottom in the corner shop opposite the Trustee Savings Bank.

"I was born in Richards Road in the early 1900s. When we were children we played cricket, rounders and marbles in the middle of the road, stopping only occasionally to let a bus go by. There were very few private cars, mostly horse driven vans and carts. It is now amusing to recall that if you were riding in the upper open top deck of the bus and it rained, you could sit there with an umbrella up. The Bus Terminus was by the Co-op Stores — Gleadless Road/Carrfield Road.

There was a big yard at the top of Richards Road where horses were stabled and loose coal sold. People bought 1 cwt or ½ cwt and it was collected in homemade wooden boxes or handcarts on 2 wheels. Sometimes an old pram would be used. If anyone had a larger quantity of coal delivered the coal dealer would tip it out on to the pavement outside the house and it was left for you to shovel the coal into your own cellar. Neighbours were very friendly and used to help, and sometimes men would follow the coal carts offering to shovel the coal into the cellars to earn a few pence. If they got 6d (2p) that was marvellous. There was a lot of unemployment in those days and men were glad to earn a few coppers which would help the family.

Mrs. Price had a house window shop at the top of Richards Road and she sold almost anything you could ask for. Where she kept all her stock in such a small place I don't know. Mrs. Reynolds had a chip shop in Spencer Road below Anns Road. She was very well known. Miss Cob had a drapery and wool shop on Anns Road and she was a very kind and helpful person. There was also a deaf and dumb cobbler on Anns Road who was a very busy man. All these were house window shops. In fact there were shops at nearly every corner of Anns Road and the roads crossing it. One wonders how they all made a living. The busiest I think was Hartley's fruit and veg shop at the corner of Alexandra Road and Anns Road.

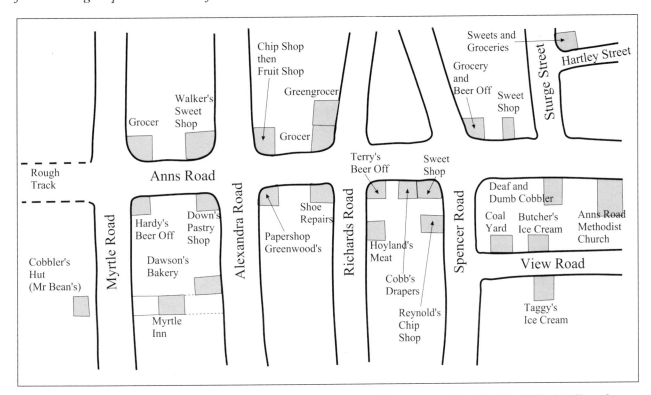

Shops on Anns Road and the surrounding streets in the 1920s and 30s as remembered by Mr Clifford Mills and Mrs Jessie Quincy

I can vaguely remember a man leading a dancing bear down the road. It was walking on its hind legs. Also a man selling slabs of salt. Salt was not sold in packets then and we had to crush it ourselves for use in the house. Milk was delivered by horse and cart and the milkman would measure the milk and pour it into your own jug. The horses were marvellous. They always knew just when to walk and stop, and were very popular with the children. The doctor's surgery was in Gleadless Road opposite the paper - shop, and the waiting room was the Caretaker's kitchen. A bit different to the Clinics we now have.

I can also remember a fair in Gerard Street at holiday times, and the Docker as it was then before any houses were built.

My mother, who was also born in Richards Road, in 1880, told me she fetched milk from a farm where the Co-op Stores now stands at the end of Carrfield Road/Gleadless Road."

Mrs. Jessie Quincey (nee Weaver)

Aubrey Langhorn in his shop on the corner of Fitzroy and Gleadless Roads. 1960s.

Joyce Jenkinson interviewed Aubrey Langhorn a few years ago. He told her that his grandfather was the yard foreman at G D Cook, Northcote Brickworks. Mr Langhorn's father Ted also worked there until it closed, when he bought the milk round from Mr Hustler of Newfield Farm, then opened his own dairy, sweets and tobacco shop at 24 Heeley Green in 1924. He built the dairy at the back of the house. They also made their own ice-cream. He used to fetch the milk from Tideswell in Derbyshire twice a day, then started to have it sent by rail and collected the churns from Heeley Station. He delivered the milk around Heeley in two churns in a cart pulled by a horse called Charlie during the years 1924 to 1942. Ted Langhorn was also the father of Edmund Langhorn who was killed in North Africa in 1943.

"From Upper Heeley Club (Abney House) we come down to Memmots at the corner of Fitzroy. Memmots, in the first instance were farmers. All land round Northcote and round there used to be called Memmots fields. There was a brickyard there, but it was not working. It had gone bust. They must have made bricks there to build houses on Northcote. I should say so because there was the brickyard in Hurlfield Hill as well. They were both in the same scheme because they both closed at the same time. Across road there was Langhorns but there was somebody before Langhorns - forget. That was provisions. I think they used to sell milk I'm not too sure but I've an idea they did. The shop next to 261 was Alice Storey's general provisions shop. We are now at the end of Fitzroy where the Church is. Then there was the chip shop at the corner of Northcote Road. Then another provisions - can't think of the name - one down Northcote Road. A little house window shop, in fact I think there was two. Then there was Hainings, the Chemist, a Newsagents (Woolhouse), Fish shop (Gaunts), Sweet shop (Holborns), and the Co-op. Rackhams were a very famous shop. She was the midwife. Poor people used to go for stock that they had boiled the pork in and take it home in jugs and Mums would add all vegetables from the allotments. Nearly everybody had a garden, if not at the back of the house then on allotments. They used to grow their own vegetables and make soups and stews.

An off-licence on Alexandra Road in the 1900s.
Sheffield Local Studies Library.

Now the shops opposite Heeley Church. There was the barbers-hairdressers. A 4oz-penny shop (Woods). There's Gower's corner shop. And I think there was a fruit shop.

Going back to Cat Lane - Mrs. Garner, she lived in Cat Lane and she used to make pastries and that and sell them from her house. Mrs. Garner was a friend of my Mother's. Mrs. Prince was her daughter. T'old lady might never have gone into shop I can't recollect that. But Mrs. Garner used to make the pastries and that, from her house. And then she had the bakehouse built. Or perhaps the daughter had it built, I don't know. I don't know whether they got married before she died or whether they had the shop built before she died. So whether it was Prince's shop in first instance or whether it was Mrs. Garner's I don't really know. This is about 1930 something. I can remember the houses being built on Cat Lane. Before that there were cottages. They were on the right hand side going down. I took that bakehouse myself, about 1952, for about 2 years. I had a little A35 Austin van. I used to go round shops supplying them with custards and fruit pies and cakes and teacakes. I used to go up Gleadless Estate as well. It carried on. Mrs. Burrows bought it. They had a bakehouse up Highfields. There was another bakehouse at the bottom of Carrfield Road, round the corner into Albert Road, called Selby's. They used to have the bakehouse in the yard at back. They were Mrs. Wilkinson's brother-in-law, and his parents.

Now Anns Road - there were two corner shops at Anns Road and Myrtle Road. There were bakehouse and sweet shop, corner of Alexandra Road and Anns Road, then there were newspapers shop and fruit shop on other corner of Alexandra Road and Anns Road. Further on there were two more shops on corner of Spencer Road. Opposite corner were a house. On the corner of Richards Road there were Gordon Lee's. Gordon Lee was Sheffield Band Leader. They called them G. Lee Band. They did G. Lee's Dances. His parents had the beer-off shop on the corner of Richards Road. We were in the same class at school. He used to go to Heeley Bank with me. Just below him in Richards Road there were Butchers, Hoylands, where my mother used to go for meat." **Eddie Chapman**

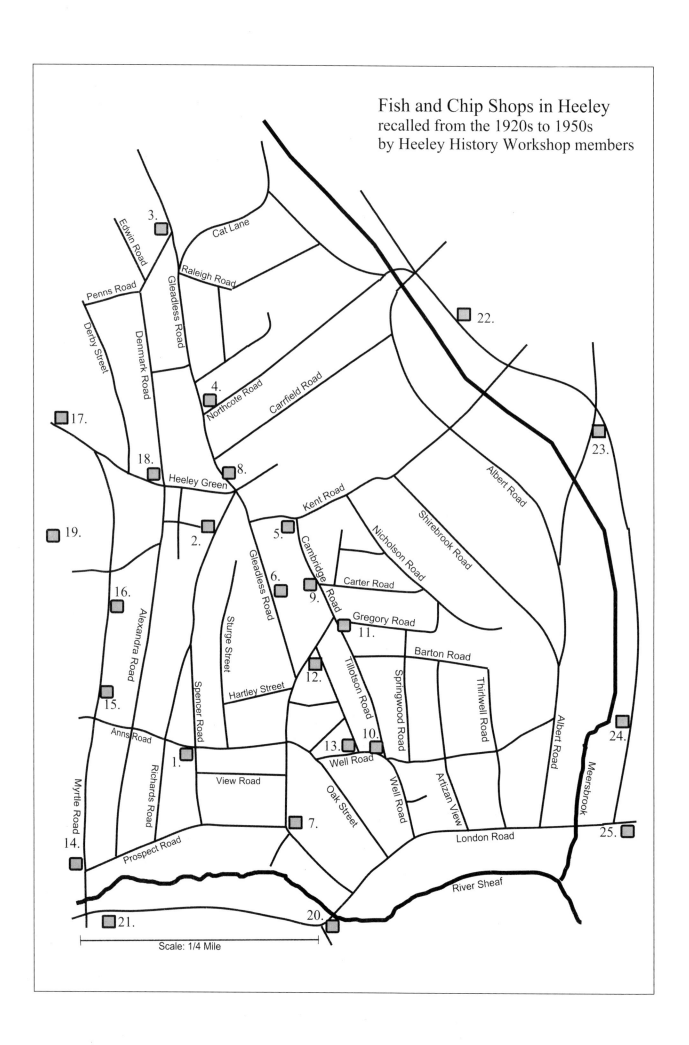

Fish and Chip Shops in Heeley
recalled from the 1920s to 1950s
by Heeley History Workshop members

1. Timperley's, later Mitchell's, house window shop on Spencer Road just below Anns Road.

2. Exton's, later Smith's from 1939, house window shop on Richards Road near Bowler Street.

3. Howard's, a house window shop on Penns Road.

4. Calver's/Elliot's, corner of Northcote and Gleadless Road.

5. A house window shop on Kent Road, just below the Waggon and Horses. Hughes, see page 8.

6. Sam Maude's, just below the Post Office near Dobb's on Gleadless Road.

7. The first recorded chip shop in Heeley, on Gleadless Road opposite Sheaf Bank opened in 1890.

8. Syke's shop, next to Haining's the chemist, on Gleadless Road.

9. Jimmy's, on Cambridge Road, opposite Carter Road.

10. Jubbs's, at the bottom of Tillotson Road.

11. Mrs Thompson's, at the corner of Tillotson and Gregory Roads.

12. A house window shop on Boyton Street, near the top.

13. Wilcock's, near the bottom of Boyton Street.

14. Barber's, then Sunset 77, on Myrtle Road, on the corner with Midhill Road.

15. A house window shop, on Myrtle Road just above Ann's Road on the right.

16. A house window shop, on Myrtle Road, just below and opposite the quarry.

17. A shop on Myrtle Road, above the Ball Inn on the same side.

18. A shop on Denmark Road at the top corner with Heeley Green.

19. A shop on East Road, half way up.

20. A shop on Broadfield Road, near the genel leading to Saxon Road

21. A shop on Queen's Road, next to the Earl of Arundel and Surrey pub.

22. Fiddler's, a house window shop, on Rushdale Road, bombed during the blitz.

23. A shop on Valley Road, just below the junction with Brooklyn Road, still there.

24. A house window shop on Valley Road, near Empire Rib.

25. Mason's, a corner shop on Windsor and Chesterfield Roads.

Shops 20 and 21 were used when coming home from football matches, shops 22 to 25 were visited on the way home from Abbeydale Picture Palace or dance hall. Mr Chapman can remember buying 1/2d worth of chips and 1d for a fish, in the 1930s the prices had risen to 1d for chips and 2d for fish.

"I enjoyed reading about Heeley and seeing in my mind's eye what it used to be like. I remember Brailsfords very well - to me as a child it was a magical place, always so clean, and the windows were lined with glass shelves and then filled with lots of tiny bottles of sweets. They sold beautiful biscuits and chocolates and their home-made potted meat was mouth watering. If I remember right it was run by two sisters. Next up the road was an opening into a large yard, the back door of Brailsfords, Rowe's Pork Shop, Bowlers Meat and Denniffs' Meat shop, which was all on London Road.

Past the yard opening was Hill's newsagents shop where you went up two steps into the shop. I can remember what a thrill it was to get my comics. I used to buy 'Chips', which was a pink paper comic, and 'Film Fun'. Next was a small sweet shop which an old lady kept - it was closed for a long time after her death, then made it into a house. Above that were two more houses, then a cobbler's shop. Well Place was the next, with houses all along one side - at the top of Well Place were the backs of some of the houses in Artisan View. Down the other side from the top were two larger type houses then a yard and another large house which was B(r)own's (?) coal merchants. Then at the bottom was Geesons shop, which was a grocery and off-licence where people used to take basins for loose piccalilli, etc., bottles for loose vinegar and jugs for beer. Next door to that up Well Road were two houses with an entry in between, then two houses, an entry and another house.

Next, all one could see was large walls with iron railings on the top and then a flight of steps leading to two front gardens and two houses - these houses stood high up above the road and they were the only two houses to have front gardens and private good-sized back gardens, plus their own toilets. At the back of these two houses was a fairly large building which had a stable, large store place and a large place over the top - this was all fastened up with large doors opening up in Well Head Road. The tenants of the two houses were given keys to all doors because it was their back way where the bin men came.

At one time we were tenants of one of these houses for about 40 years and we were the tenants of the stable and buildings, first my grandparents then my parents. We were meat deliverers. My father used to own a horse and cart and it was my thrill to go to work with him Saturday mornings - we used to go to the abattoir to collect meat, but first we went to Pond Hill to the Ice Stores to collect large blocks of ice which were put on the cart before collecting meat - it kept the meat cool; also to deliver ice as well to the butcher's shop for their own ice boxes. We also used to deliver blocks of ice to Granelli's where we would always get our cups full of ice cream.

My father's horse was a large cart-horse - he was called Bob. He was brown with white markings. He was so tame and gentle I used to ride him bare back when after work on Saturday we used to take him from the stable on Goodwin Road (which is still there, or was the last time I went on there). I used to show off a bit by standing on his back along Gleadless Road - people used to look at me but they didn't realise that his back. was so large and he was so gentle it was as safe as being on a table, but it looked good. My Dad used to take him to the farm to let him have his freedom in one of their fields for the weekend in the good weather. He used to go into the field, chase around it then start rolling in the grass, he always made me laugh. I don't really know how long we had him, it seems to be all the time. I can't remember us not having a horse as a child. About 1936 my father let Bob go to a circus - he exchanged him for one of their show horses. This horse was a complete opposite - it was a beautiful black mare with a white star on her forehead, she used to pull the cart, lifting up her legs rather like she has always been taught to do in her work in the circus. This horse had been over-trained and had kicked her trainer who was getting afraid of her, but my Dad bought her. Gone were my days of riding bare back as I was frightened of her. If anyone but my Dad went into the stable she used to snort and kick out high with either her front legs or back (whichever was the nearest to her foes). My Dad loved her and was so proud of her when he went out with her, no one dare go near her or the dray when he was out at work.

In 1938 my Dad heard that the shops he used to deliver to on Shalesmoor and around that area, were being demolished so my Dad sold his dray and his beloved mare "Bess". He told the two-men who bought her and the dray that she was good now but they mustn't use a whip of any kind on her, just to speak gently to her and she would always oblige. He even went for two days with them on their work, saying nothing, just watching and being there while she got used to them but alas a couple of weeks after she killed herself and the man driving, by going through a brick wall. My Dad was so upset it took him months to get over it and if he'd only waited, the war was declared in 1939 so the shops were not pulled down, he lost a good round of shops and all the trade he'd built up. The other man got in touch with my Dad saying that his mate did use the whip and wouldn't take any heed to him when he tried to stop him.

I think he got the hay, straw, from the farm at the bottom of Hurlfield Hill where we took both horses. The manure was given to Mr. Houseman (I think that's what he was called) who used to live at the top house over the wall in the first yard up the top half of Artisan View. He used to pass his buckets over and my Dad and anyone, including me, used to fill them, then pass them back over the wall. He used to give us beautiful flowers, vegetables, and tomatoes, etc. so it worked very well for them both. The cart was a flat dray and we had a boxed seat at the front where we sat. I think it was green painted with a thin gold line down the edge. My Dad kept the stable above and he also kept fowls. Mr. Cardwell was well known in Heeley. He eventually took over our former stable in Well Head Road. He dealt in second-hand goods and he was there many years. I think he came into the stable in the 1930's just before the war.

Further up Well Road still, large walls continued to another flight of steps and above were two more houses, then Newcombe's sweets, grocery and off licence and they owned the next building which came on Well Head Road, which was a Dairy. Mr. Newcombe was called Tom and he used to deliver milk in a Tate & Lyle Sugar box with pram wheels attached and he had quite a good round about Heeley so a lot of people must still remember this. The milk came in large churns and the milkman carried measures to pour the milk out of it into his customers' jugs or basins, etc. Later on he got a motor bike with a wooden box on the side to carry the churns. The milk was collected from Heeley station (where the scrap yard is now). It used to come from farms from Hathersage, Bamford, Clay Cross, etc.

The road went bending now and the next place was at the bottom of Tillotson Road and it was a hairdresser and later on a greengrocery. Stevensons sweet shop was at the bottom of Boynton Street. Across from Stevensons was Fletchers chips and fish shop and it was well known, for people used to queue at this shop sometimes over half an hour, they were so delicious. Next up Well Road were all houses, then a sweet and grocery shop which practically came on to Hyde Road. Next came a pie and pea shop, then two houses and finally the Shakespeare Public house. I should mention that opposite the Shakespeare public house was a large wall and behind was a large area of uncultivated ground stretching down to the first shops going down this part of Gleadless Road which was Taggy's ice-cream shop.

Coming down Well Road from the Shakespeare from the other side was another Public House which started at the top of Oak Street, then about three houses, an entry and another three houses. Then three more houses, an entry and three more houses. Next came Kendall's yard and house - they had a woodturner's workshop. Below came three back-to-back houses. The front three houses came directly on to the pavement but there was an entry to the back of these and they had a garden and the toilet block where each back-to-back house shared a toilet. On the opposite side of this entry was Stacey's fruit and sweet shop where I can remember going for $^1/2$d peanuts, 5 palm toffees for 1 old pence, and 2 old pence of pot herbs - these usually used to be 1 onion, 2 carrots and a small turnip. Then came the hairdresser's shop, next was a house, then another shop which was Fry's - they used to sell tripe, cow-heels, and home-made bakery. These last four houses were all tenanted by one family - Nora had the baker's shop, Barbara lived next door, Olive had the hairdressers and Annie had the greengrocery - they were all sisters. The four sisters were all married. No. 33 Well Road was the tripe, bakers shop, and she was called Nora Fry. She used to bake her own bread cakes and pastries every day. Her husband was well

known as a painter and sign writer, he was called Sydney. He did a lot of work in certain cinemas and as his daughter, Barbara was my best friend, we never went short of complementary tickets to visit the pictures. Barbara lives now in Albert Road and she had a brother called Rodney. Next door, at 35 was Barbara Bolton - this was just a house. Her husband was called John - he was an electrician. I think they had only two boys, David and Gary. At 37 was a house-window shop but the daughter Olive Powell, made it into a hairdresser's shop. She had one daughter called Olive, also. Next was the sweets and greengrocery shop - this had one shop window then the doorway, then a small house window, the sister here was called Annie and her husband was called Percy. They had one daughter who lived with her husband for many years in Artisan View. The sisters' maiden name was Whitehead and their parents lived at No. 37 until their death.

Next was an entry to three buildings - the first two were houses. The bottom one was Harrisons - this shop was very small and I often, as a child, used to stand spell-bound by this shop, it was so old-fashioned; to describe it best is to imagine it in York Museum for when I go there I always think of Harrisons. It was run by an old lady who was very polite but this shop seemed to be untouched by time. Next came three back-to-back houses then an entry and three more back-to-back houses. At the top of the yard were toilets so again two houses shared one toilet. Next was Hill's toyshop - a thrill again for me - it was like Aladdin's cave for us children. Hills owned the newsagents opposite as well and they lived in the large house below the Post Office and shops on Albert Road. Below Hills was an open yard to three more houses where a deaf and dumb lady lived - she always seemed to be at the top of this yard and everyone used to wish her Good-day, etc. Then there was a greengrocery shop and a Herbalist, then came part of the Heeley Palace.

There was a well in our front cellar. The walls of our cellar were very thick and one side was cut out like a big shelf with cut-outs in the brick wall. The ceiling was made of stone and the opposite corner was the well. My Dad remembered it open as when my Grandmother lived there she used to use it but when my Mother took over the house she got my Father to put a large stone slab over it so I never saw it open but if we had a heavy rain storm or heavy snow, the lady who lived next door used to complain that water was in her cellar but we could hear only water running under the slab into the well so ours was always dry. There was also a well (past Skinner's Builders' yard) up Artisan View just outside the back door of Number 42, where Mr. Newcombe's son used to live.

On London Road from the corner of Well Road was Brailsfords at the corner. Bowlers next shop, Rowe's pork butchers. There was Denniffs meat shop, a shop which sold all sorts of eggs including foreign eggs, then an entry to the houses at the back, then the public house and then King's bacon shop which came at the bottom of Artisan View. Opposite the next corner of Artisan View was Wood's Mens Outfitters and hairdressers, then was a meat shop and Sorby's fish shop, then bakers and Phillips's pork shop. Next, was Beecraft's hardware. This shop was very long and full of all sorts of smells from the different soap's and powders, etc. I can't remember what was on the corner, all I can recall was it was a car salesroom. Across the bottom of Thirlwell Road was the Red Lion public house, the same as now. I can't recall the shops next but on the corner was a large grocery shop. It was quite old-fashioned - every bag of sugar, dried fruit, etc. was wrapped in blue bags." **Mrs. Marie Gregory, nee Reynolds**

"I spent my childhood in Tillotson Road. Our family took over the tenancy of a house, No.52, when the previous occupant, Constable Young, moved to Springwood Road in 1901. I understand that the ten stone houses, divided into two groups of five, each group with an entrance passage, were the first to be built in 1874 by a Mr. Tillotson, a wealthy landowner, who insisted that the residents must be teetotal. The name "Temperance View" puzzled me for many years until some kind soul told me what the word "temperance" meant. Our milkman was Mr. Lamb, who had a dairy in Springwood Road. Mr. Bottomley, who also lived in Springwood Road, delivered milk to many Heeley customers. He was a kind old man, who, aware of my keen interest in goldfish, invited me to look at his fish tanks. I always remember his visits, how his hand shook as he poured the milk from his big jug into our bowl. I admit I was sometimes disappointed when he never spilled a drop on the table. I became a member of the "Tillotson Road Gang" - an innocent collection of lads, at an early age. We had our "headquarters" in a cellar which Mr. Lamb used as a secondary dairy. Apparently it had served many purposes in its long lifetime, a bakery for instance.

As I cast my mind back over the years, I recall many interesting people. Mr. Musgrave, the grocer who always wore a hard hat. Mrs. Thompson, the chip shop lady with short cut hair. A formidable lady - "straight up and down" as a neighbour described her. She once heard a boy tell his mate that "he'd knock that salt pot o'er". Her reply was short and swift "Watch me knock thy hee—ad off!". No one dared to ask when she had few customers, whether she had any chips left. An affirmative reply would have inevitably invited the response "You shouldn't have made so many.

The green grocer was a Mr. Hingley, who had a wonderful horse which I used to feed with crusts of bread. Our neighbour, George Wright, a man of many skills, worked for a milkman and himself made ice-cream in his front room. We always knew that Maggie Hall would allow us to play in her large back yard. However, we also knew that old Grannie Smith was a different kettle of fish. She had a keen sense of hearing and possibly of smell, because she would appear at her front door and shout across the road "Don't bother kicking that ball about it will break my window!" before we had even bounced the thing. Really at heart she was a kind old lady, whose husband, a grinder, had been killed at work. Her granddaughter, May Bell, now a patient in Blenheim Nursing Home, was my piano teacher.

Our family remained in the house until 1971, when the house was demolished. Dad had lived there from the age of eight. I think that the shock of removal helped to shorten his life, for he died in 1972. Happy memories playing marbles in the gutter, games in the old wash house at the top of the garden and my lifelong friendship with Lol Staples, who was five days older than me and who lived at No. 60."
A. Montgomery

Cambridge Road in the 1960s. *Sheffield Local Studies Library.*

"One of my early memories is going up Cambridge Road, just above Carter Road and giving a ha'penny to a man with two birds in a cage, he made them sing by winding them up, then he would give two sweets to those who had paid, there was always a lot of kids, but a ha'penny was a lot in those days. Another thing I remember, it must have been the winter of 1947 when the snow had been on the ground about three weeks, because when the roads had been cleared I remember walking to school on top of the piles of snow in the edge of the road. I lived in Midland Road. All the houses had cellars and I was terrified of going down there for coal as there was no light. Then the cellar was made into an air raid shelter with strong wooden beams and electric light, somewhere to play when it rained. At the end of Midland Road on the right hand side going towards Tillotson Road was a grocery shop, opposite that another house window shop, below that was a big yard. The family who lived there ran a horse and cart and sold green groceries but they didn't come round that area. I think they were called Hingleys but I am not sure. Every now and then I used to go and clean the stall out and brush the horse down with a brush in each hand, I had to stand on a box, the horse looked so big to me, but I'm sure he used to sigh just like a dog when his back was scratched. I got two or three bruised apples, but I liked doing it. Another horse and cart used to come round Middle Heeley and the cart had blow up tyres and all of us kids used to hang around looking and stroking the horse.

On the left hand side of Midland Road on the corner of Tillotson Road was another shop selling greens just past the shop down Tillotson Road was another yard up a narrow entrance but as you went in on your left were some steps leading to a dairy, I think it was Newcombe's before they went to Artisan View. As you went in it opened up into a big yard with some sort of warehouses on the left which went under the back yards of Midland Road, I always wanted to look in them but I did not dare. The fruit shop was called Kay's, later Russell. I used to go somewhere up Heeley Green for clogs and when the irons had worn down a bit I could have some hobnails put in. I used to love walking about in them — but you couldn't sneak up on anyone." **D Hague**

For 44 years Pat Ann Hair was a popular hairdressing salon in Heeley. Opening in 1958 at 18 Bradwell Street the business moved in 1972 to 182 Alexandra Road. Ann Patrica Grooby was the owner and manager, her daughters Ann (now Dolby) and Claire (now Sawyer) assisting as stylists. The shop closed in June 2000.

Joyce Jenkinson remembered that her cousin Winnie Wright (already mentioned in connection with VE Day in a previous chapter) used to work at the Sheffield and Ecclesall Co-operative Society store at the corner of Carrfield and Gleadless Roads. She worked in the Drapery Department for several years during the 1940s. Ron Eaton worked in the Butchery Department then volunteered for the navy during the war. After four and a half years he was demobbed. Winnie and Ron were married in Heeley Parish Church in 1949 and now live at Gleadless.

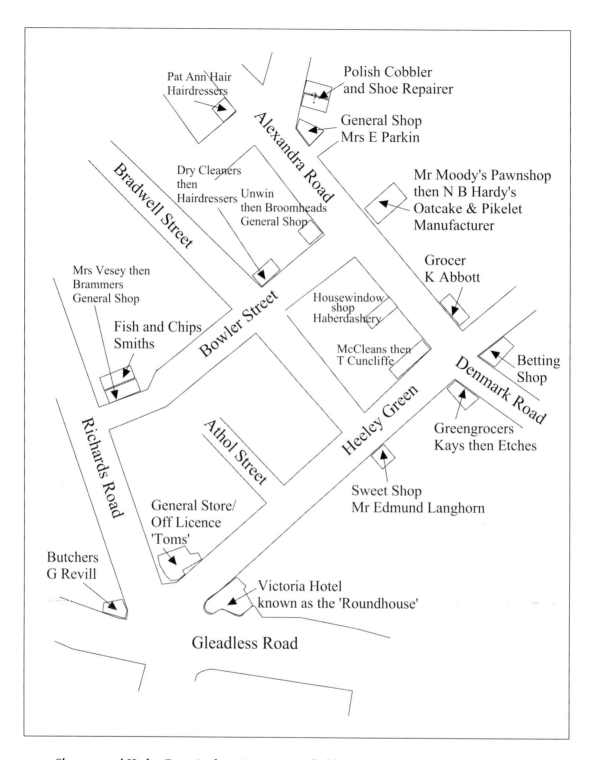

Shops around Heeley Green in the 1950 to 70s recalled by Ann Dolby and members of her family.

"*The Heeley Branch of the S&E Co-op was Number 2 of all the shops they opened in Sheffield. Number 1 was the Main Arcade at the bottom of Ecclesall Road. [Where Safeway is now.] As a child I always thought it had been there a very long time, but Mr Chapman tells me that originally the Co-op was on the corner of Forster Road and Gleadless Road opposite Heeley Parish Church. When the larger Co-op was built on the site of Mettam's farm at the corner of Carrfield Road and Gleadless Road the old shop was taken over by Gower's. My mother did most of her shopping at the Co-op, there was a grocery store, a drapery store and shoe department and the butcher's department.*

Each department had a strong cable going through a hole in the wall to the cashiers' desk in the main grocery store, along with the little metal canisters were sent back and forth from the sales counters to the cashier which the payment or change or dividend checks. The grocery store was a hive of activity - if there were few shoppers in then the assistants would be busy weighing out sugar into blue bags, currants or raisins into red bags, flour into muslin bags or balm (yeast) into 2d packets. I think this was for 1oz weight. They would pat butter or margarine into brick shaped slabs.

Gleadless Road, looking down Forster Road. Sheffield Local Studies Library.

The draper's shop had a long counter with a brass measure fitted along one edge. If you asked for one yard of ribbon the assistant would open up one of the little drawers, pull out a spool of the appropriate shade and with lightening hand movements would extend the end of the ribbon along the measure, snip the ribbon with scissors, roll it up and pop it in a small brown paper bag. Almost as quickly she would measure out two yards of material for a Whit Sunday dress, match the colour with a reel of Sylko and accept some stamps from the Whitsun club card in payment for it. You had to go through the drapery shop to get to the shoe shop.

The butchery department was always colder than all the other shops, its door open, sawdust on the floor and the storeroom at the far end cold with ice blocks and hanging meat carcasses draped in white strawclothes. Mr Cartledge, the butcher, greeted us like old friends. 'Two rabbits did you say? Do you want them skinning? Would you like me to chop them up for you? That's 8d for this one and 9d for that, one and five pence please.' The butcher's boy would deliver your meat for you to the door on his bicycle, and the grocery department would deliver your order free if you took your order book in early enough – initially by horse and cart and later by van. Such personal service went by the board with the opening of supermarkets." **Lilian Haywood.**

"In this age of supermarkets of the ilk of Tesco, Sainbury's and Asda the heyday of the corner shop seems alas to be past. In Heeley a few linger on, but to walk along Ann's Road today, for instance, is to see the grim evidence of their demise. To retrace one's steps to fifty years ago and walk along that same road would be to find shops on almost every corner. No less than three off-licences or 'Beer Offs', a butcher's, bakery, newsagents and fruitshop flourished there all providing a personal service, where friends and neighbours often met and swapped gossip. Now, not a single shop remains. All have been demolished and replaced by new housing, open spaces and the area of Heeley City Farm. Where, one might ask, are the likes of the Drakes, Greenwoods and Downs, those shopkeepers of old, today?

Recently I returned to the Olive Grove area of Heeley, where I had lived for nearly forty years, specifically to see if any of the local corner shops there has survived. I was not surprised by what I found. How things had changed! The whole of Olive Grove, part of Spurr Street and Slate Street had become one way streets and the only sign of a corner shop was what I remembered as Beresford's then Newboult's which had been a grocers. It was shuttered and surrounded by scaffolding, obviously it had not functioned as a shop for a long time. At the other end of Olive Grove Road, the building which had been the Sheffield and Ecclesall Co-operative Stores and the largest shop in the area was now James House, No. 11, Midhill Road. Much to my amazement it appeared to have been converted into flats! I recalled the early days, when as a small girl, I was fascinated by *the little metal cups which zoomed overhead along wires carrying cash and change to and from the cashiers. When older I had gone each Friday to hand in our weekly grocery order and buy our milk tokens for the milkman to collect when he delivered our milk.*

I continued to the corner of Delf Street and Spurr Street where Mr Fowkes, for as many years as I could remember, had had his grocer's shop. This had been very large and high ceilinged. A stern faced man, I had been a little in awe of him and preferred to be serve by Emily or 'Emmie' his live in assistant of longstanding, who not only worked in the shop but also, despite a pronounced limp, often delivered orders on foot. I found that the shop had undergone a complete transformation and was now an elegant private house. The conversion had completely erased any traces of Mr Fowkes' shop so that even the original doorway had disappeared.
I had kept the best until last. Finally I came to 'my corner shop' at the top of the ginnel on Slate Street - the wide alleyway which linked it with Olive Grove Road. Sellars' shop originally had been an ordinary end kitchen house in a yard of four, as indeed, it has become again. For me it epitomised all that a corner shop should be. When first I knew him, the owner of the shop, George Sellars, ran a newspaper delivery round from his home in Spurr Street. Quite a character, he was a familiar figure as he personally delivered papers twice daily, morning and evening around the neighbourhood. When the previous occupiers retired George and his wife took over the shop and this soon became their proud domain. Continuing as a newsagents, his business was soon expanding in all directions. Living quarters were at the back and the front room, which formed the shop, had shelves crammed with all manners of goods: sweets, cigarettes, dried goods, patent medicines, haberdashery, cleaning materials, stationery – the list is endless. You name it, he had it! Whatever you wanted George seemed to stock. Even when the shop suffered damage in the blitz, George could proudly boast, 'We never close!' as he continued to run his business temporarily serving his customers from a hut in the backyard. One end of the shop he converted into a lending library, an added bonus for me. My mother was an avid reader and many of the novels she read I read too. She was particularly fond - as I was – of the historical romances of John Jeffrey Farnol, all borrowed from Sellars' lending library.
Sadly George Sellars is long gone, dying whilst in harness in his early fifties of a heart attack, brought on, dare I suggest, by overwork and excessive smoking. His sudden death shocked the neighbourhood. I tell his story now for he is typical of all the hardworking little shopkeepers who are a dying breed. I remember him with affection, for it is perhaps, thanks to him and his little cornershop that my love affair with history began."
Betty Renshaw.

Some firms in Heeley such as Ponsford's (page 52) have continued in business for generations, Dawson's Pikelets on Alexandra Road are one example of such a family business.
"FLIP, flip, goes John Dawson. "Oatcakes are the ultimate" flip, flip "in fast lines" flip, flip "in a bakery." It takes hardly more than a minute to make an oat cake in his firm's premises in Alexandra Road, Heeley. Opposite Heeley City Farm, it hasn't moved from the site since great, great, grandma Annie Dawson started making them over 100 years ago.
John, fifth generation oatcake maker and flipper, starts at 4.30am by making the batter, a mix of white and brown flour, oatmeal, water, salt, sodium bicarbonate and a little yeast. It bubbles away, fermenting gently, for half an hour. Then blobs of batter are dropped on to the 15ft long steel, gas-fired hot plate. He now makes seven dozen at a time with a hand-held hopper, pressing a plunger to deliver a measured amount. The batter spreads into a circle and cooks, the holes produced by the bicarb releasing carbon dioxide. Then each little golden, glowing, lacy sun is flipped by hand with a paint scraper to cook on the other side. It's a wonder John doesn't suffer from repetitive strain injury. He left school at 15 and has been making them ever since. He's 48. John used to work with his younger brother Peter who has since left to run a shop so it's now a one man and his mum business. Jean lays them on a rack to cook then bags them four at a time. Oatcakes, the British version of a chapatti, if you think about it traditionally go well fried with bacon and eggs but are equally as good toasted and spread with butter and jam. It may be a food from the past but is very much the food of today with no fat, no sugar and lots of fibre. But so far John hasn't persuaded any of the big supermakets to take them. Instead, he sets out each morning in his little van and delivers to shops around the city. The sign on the factory, little more than a couple of rooms in an old house, also proclaims E Dawson & Sons are pikelet makers. "I call them crumpets now to avoid any confusion. They are virtually the same as oatcakes but without the oatmeal and are made in little moulds," he says. He makes around 25,000 oatcakes and pikelets, sorry crumpets, a week, working every day, Sundays not excepted. Oatcakes have a short shelf life but freeze well. Young people take to them as a fast food and that's a saving grace for John. "Older people tend to buy them only in winter and stop buying in May. I suppose they used to toast them in front of the coal fire. The youngsters eat them all year round." Sheffield Star April 18th 1998.

Transport

A horse bus travelling along London Road at Heeley Bottom.
Sheffield Local Studies Library.

From 1852 there were horse-drawn trams along Heeley Bottom as far as the Red Lion. The horses were stabled at the bottom of Albert Road. Later there was an electric tram service to Woodbank Crescent and Woodseats. Even with electrification the trams could not travel up the steep hills of Heeley. The first motor bus service up to Heeley Green and beyond started in the 1930s. The earliest buses used on this route did not stop between Havelock Bridge and Heeley Green because it was difficult to restart them on the steep hill.

An advertisement in a Sheffield newspaper in 1852 researched by Sid Wetherill reads,
"Omnibus – on Monday, January 19th 1852, Mr John Shortridge intends to commence Running an Omnibus from the Royal Hotel, near the New Market, Sheffield, to Heeley, for the accommodation of the Public on the South side of the Town. The Fare to be charged is Threepence for all or any part of the way. Parcels and messages carefully delivered along the line of the Route on equally low terms; and by strict attention to time and civility, Mr Shortridge trusts that he will obtain the support of the Public. The Route will be up the Old Haymarket, and High street, Fargate, Norfolk Row, Norfolk street, Union street, and South street."

The steep gradients of Heeley roads have always made haulage difficult. There were ways of making the work easier for horses. *"One coal man used to fetch coal from the Heeley sidings, and when he got to the bottom of Hurlfield Hill he used to take some of the coal off the dray, prop it at the side of the wall, and take the horse up with about 6 bags on, because Hurlfield Hill was like that, and it could only get up with about 6 bags, then come down again, and his 6 bags of coal would still be there. There would be no vandalism in them days, you know. Hurlfield Hill was notoriously dangerous for cyclists, more than one having lost control of his bike on the way down."* HHW

Draymen often took a 'pull-up' horse, i.e. a spare horse fastened behind the dray which could be reharnessed at the front to help the regular horse pull up steep places. *"Corporation always had one at the bottom of Havelock Bridge waiting to bring the dust carts up to Olive Grove."* Horses were kept at Lowfield to help haul the horse trains to Highfield, a lad in charge bringing them down again. Myrtle Road was considered steep, *"but they managed 'to get up there with one horse, with coal and things like that, and of course every ten or twenty yards there was a block of stone at the edge of the footpath (about 1 or 2 feet high) and they would take the cart up and when they got to that piece of stone they let it rest there, and then it would have another go to the next piece of stone and they would wedge it again, until they finally got to the top."*
Eddie Chapman

It was reckoned that a horse could pull a ton. Sometimes a pull-up horse was needed, *"but could the people afford to have one? It had to go up whether it liked it or not. Some of them used to fall down because they were hungry."* In frosty weather they might fall and be unable to get up. *"They used to put sacking down, didn't they and try to get them up? But they didn't grit roads like now. People were responsible for clearing snow from the paths outside their houses. The policeman would tell people to get it done. People used ashes from the coal fires to spread on slippery places."* HHW

For the first thirty years of the twentieth century there was relatively little mechanised transport. The roads were busy with a variety of wheeled vehicles, the likes of which are rarely seen today. Some trades people had hand carts like rag and bone men who gave donkey stone or gold fish in exchange for old clothes and bones from meat joints. Some carts were used for deliveries such as meat like Tesh, who parked his outside the Waggon and Horses on Gleadless Road or Johnny Ice Cream Man or Butcher's who were based in a house window shop in View Road. Some hand cart users such as Ponsfords went

on to other means of transport. The hand cart used by the founder of Ponsfords is still proudly displayed in the back of their shop on London Road. Arnold Laver soon outgrew his original store yard in Heeley and his hand cart, replacing it with a motor bike and side car before moving to Bramall Lane in the 1920s. Taggy's ice cream moved on from hand carts to vans but Wall's 'Stop Me and Buy One' bicycles were still in use in the days of many of our members.

Vans and cars on London Road in the 1948.
Sheffield Local Studies Library.

Railway and brewery drays were pulled by big horses. Breweries were the first to use traction engines, steam traction. In 1914 lorries were beginning to come into Sheffield, but horse-drawn transport was common well into the 1930s. Only better off people could afford cabs. One member recalled being taken to Heeley station in a horse-drawn cab in the 1920s to catch a train to Bridlington. Taxis were not common.

"Thomas Wilkinson, the builder, he always used to ride about chauffeur driven when he got a car, but I remember him being in a horse and carriage once, but I can only just remember. Old man Thomas Wilkinson, he had a beard, portly fellow, and he had a Heeley fellow called Pemberton, and Tom Pemberton was a driver, and all his late years he used to drive Mr. Thomas Wilkinson about in his car." HHW

Many butchers had bicycles for the delivery of their joints by butcher's boys on Saturdays, and some shops received their meat and ice for storing it by horse and cart. A lot of milk and coal was delivered by horse and cart. The firm of Hukin in Thirlwell Road, now run by the fifth generation of the family, delivered coal and yeast by horse and cart for over 120 years. Mr Chapman's grandfather, Mr Ibberson had a pony and cart, stabled near his shop on the corner of Wright's Row up Heeley Green, a lot of his deliveries were in the Park area.

A group of women and children setting off on a Charabanc outing from outside the Sheakespeare Inn in the 1920s.

Old prams were very much in demand for collecting shopping like a stone of flour for bread making or for collecting a bag of coal from the coal yard or chopped up wood for lighting fires. Men with allotment gardens would often be seen pushing wheelbarrows containing home-grown produce, bags of potatoes, onions or big cabbages. These were always home-made ones – a big wooden box (Hutton's Soap boxes were very popular) with two big wheels, usually from an old mangle and a piece of wood attached at the front to support it when rested on the ground when filling or emptying it. Two more pieces would be attached to the sides projecting backwards for handles. Any other spare wheels were usually taken over by the boys who would make go-karts for riding fast down hill – until you were collared by someone to go shopping, fetch wood or coal or for some other carrying job.

Sunday School trips and outings were very popular with all involved. Trips might have been by train or charabanc such as the one in this picture. The occasion of this outing is not known to us, can anyone help with the name of the group or suggest why only women and children seem to be taking part?

"Heeley Station brings back happy memories of outings into Derbyshire during the 1930's. There were Sunday School outings from Heeley Wesley. On one occasion we caught the train at Heeley Station about 2 o'clock to go to Hathersage. The train journey itself quite an adventure, especially through the Totley tunnel to Grindleford, in the dark. We played games in a field which surrounds the present open-air swimming pool. There was a pool there in which we could paddle, but it was just a large stretch of water in a field. We had a picnic tea, bread, fillings and buns bought from J .W. Collins, confectioners and bakers of West Street. Mr. and Mrs. Collins with their family of eight or nine children (Iris, Daisy, Pansy, Myrtle and the boys) were members of the Church.

On another occasion we went to Grindleford, where we played in the field beside the Methodist Chapel (on the left hand side before the bridge over the river, I think it is still there). It was a glorious summer's day. The train home was packed with day trippers from Hope and Hathersage when it arrived at Grindleford station. We pushed the children in, then two of we young teachers pretended we couldn't t get in and enjoyed a lovely walk home over Padley Wood through Longshaw, then over the moors past the smoke cutlets from the tunnel, to the bus at Cross Scythes, Totley." A.E. Knight

A discussion about Heeley Station evoked these memories from our members.

Heeley Bridge and the entrance to the Station in the 1960s. Sheffield Local Studies Library.

"One day my uncle was walking on the pavement under the railway when a train passed overhead. The driver chose that moment to release the water (it was a steam train) and my uncle got drenched. His suit was ruined but he put in a claim to the railway and got compensation." **Gladys Wilkinson.**

"A lot of Sheffield Wednesday supporters used to get a train from Heeley Station to Wadsley Bridge Station to watch a Saturday afternoon match. I remember going that way from time to time from 1912 up to and through the 1920s." **Eddie Chapman.**

" A lot of pigeon fanciers used to take baskets of pigeons down to Heeley Station to put on certain trains, the pigeons would be released on reaching their destination and the baskets returned to Heeley on another train."
"Yes, I remember a man who was a coffin maker. He used to keep pigeons and you could always tell when he had entered his pigeons for a race because he used to load his pigeon basket on the coffin trolley to wheel them down to the station."

"At the beginning of the last war, the evacuee children were collected together at the school playground, then they walked down to Heeley Station to get on the trains which were to take them to their foster homes."
Miss Knight.

"There used to be a lot of evening trips from Heeley Station. I remember going to Rhyl for 3/6 return and you could go to Blackpool illuminations for 2/6. You could get a ticket to Belle Vue which admitted you to the zoo for no extra charge, these tickets were 5/-." **Joan Palfreyman.**

Heeley Today

Since the house clearances of the 1970s Heeley has had a lot of empty spaces, cleared for the 'Heeley Bypass', the road that never was. Many families left the area when their terraced streets were demolished; communities like those we have described in previous chapters were uprooted. New housing was built on many of the cleared sites but very few native Heeleyites were re-housed there. Heeley is now multi-cultural; the Methodist Chapels on Anns Road and Thirlwell Road are a Chinese Christian Church and the Makki mosque respectively. Heeley has a relatively high unemployment rate compared to some other parts of Sheffield. At the last count the population was over 15,000. Many of the incomers now living in Heeley are becoming increasingly involved in a new community that has grown up.

One of the earliest schemes to reuse the derelict land was the Heeley City Farm, established in the early eighties through schemes involving the work and involvement of Heeley young people. In 1995 the Farm suffered a devastating setback when a fire swept through the complex destroying offices and stables. The White Horse of Heeley unveiled on the hillside above the Sheaf View pub is partly in commemoration of Barney, one of the horses which died as a result of the fire. This year the Farm began construction of 'the most environmentally friendly building in Sheffield'. It will be powered by sun and wind and will provide 'accommodation' for wild creatures on its plant-covered roofs!

Heeley Development Trust
The Lancelott Wall, Sheaf Bank Works, Prospect Rd, Sheffield S2 3EN
Tel 0114 250 0613 Fax 0114 258 1919 e-mail: heeleydevtrust@btinternet.com

The Heeley Development Trust was set up by local people to obtain funding to develop and manage local regeneration projects. Its aims are to act as a management and development agency for new projects, co-ordinate social and economic regeneration in the area, improve the environment of Heeley and Lowfield, reduce local unemployment (especially youth unemployment) by providing training, job creation and the establishment of community enterprises, create an information and resource agency for the area and promote community safety within the area.

One of the Trust's most visible projects has been the Heeley Millennium Park. Begun in February 1998, Phase 1 of the project consisted of earth moving in the area between Prospect Road and View Road, christened Taggy's Field. Heeley History Workshop members did inform the Heeley Development Trust that Taggy originally had his field near the junction of Daresbury and Gleadless Roads, up towards Newfield Green. But the name has stuck no doubt due to the popularity of the well-loved ice cream manufacturers. Phase 2 of the Park was laid out in November 1998 in the area between Well Road, Oak Street and the Phase 1 site. Paths and benches were added and hundreds of native trees and bulbs were planted by school children. The new playground is a major attraction in the area and one of the reasons for the popularity of the park has been that local people especially young people have had a large say in what goes into it. When large pieces of masonry were turned up by the JCBs they were shown to the Trust and were discovered to have been part of the Oak Street Methodist Chapel that had previously stood on the site. The stones have been used to make a decorative edging to some borders. The outdoor climbing boulder, a first in Sheffield, is also very popular with children and adults alike. A mosaic bench and the giant White Horse of Heeley are only two of the features added to the park in recent months. Phase 3 was begun in March 2000, between Albert Road and Goodwin Road. There has been a lot of trouble with Japanese Knotweed on this part of the site. A problem shared by the Friends of Heeley Churchyard who are cleaning and tidying their site on a regular voluntary basis.

The Trust also works with young people. Different types of work have been carried out including, young people organising their own events and trips. Also the team has given out advice and information on many areas, including, substance misuse advice and sexual heath information. A scheme has been set up to connect unemployed people with local jobs, by registering their skills. Steps have been taken to provide Information Technology training in the area and to target it at age groups, such as the over 50s, who would normally miss out on such opportunities.

Current projects that the Trust is working on:

The New Heeley Voice - A local newsletter with over 4000 copies delivered to local businesses and people's homes.

River Sheaf Project - a regeneration project for the River Sheaf corridor focusing on environmental improvements and access creation on the River Sheaf

Hartley Street Project and Enterprise Centre - community meeting/training room and rent-a-desk spaces plus development of the Hartley St Project to regenerate this derelict providing community enterprise space and other facilities.

Sheaf Valley Development Framework - a starting point for an inclusive regeneration framework for the Sheaf Valley

The Institute Building Hartley St - The Trust has managed to attract a substantial amount of Heritage Lottery Funding to re-furbish this derelict building and bring it back into use. The building will be re-built in the original style with great detail being paid to maintaining the simplicity and character of the interior, while opening it up with disabled access and toilets. Our architects have worked closely with Heritage Lottery who are obviously keen to capture the historical value of the building. The building belongs to the church in the guise of the Sheffield Diocesan Board of Finance and the Heeley Development Trust working closely with Heeley Christchurch to move the project forward by leasing the building. The re-furbished space will be available for local groups and organisations to use for meetings, events and training.

Looking down Oak Street across Phase 2 of the Millennium Park. This was the corner where The Sportsman Inn used to be. (see the picture on page 27)

Further Reading

For the Introduction

Armitage Harold (1910) *Chantrey Land*. Reprinted 1998 by Applebaum, Sheffield.

Booker AW (1939) *A History of Heeley Wesley Chapel* Private Publication

Crossley David et al (Eds) (1989) *Water Power on the Sheffield Rivers*. Sheffield Trades History Society.

Odom Rev W (1917) *Fifty Years of Sheffield Church Life*. JW Northend. Sheffield

Tatton Henry *Henry Tatton's Notebook*. A compilation of his notes and drawings available in the Sheffield Local Studies Library.

Vickers JE (1979) *Old Sheffield Town*. Applebaum. Sheffield

For Rural to Industrial

Hey David (1996) *The Oxford Companion to Local and Family History* Oxford University Press, Oxford

Trade Directories and Census Enumerators' Books for Sheffield and Heeley in Sheffield Local Studies Library and Archives.

Houseley Herbert ( ) *Back to the Grindstone*

Jones Melvyn (1989) *Sheffield's Woodland Heritage* Sheffield City Libraries.

Marron Peter (1990) *Ancient Woodland: Woodland Heritage Nature Conservancy Council* David and Charles.

For Pubs

Lamb Douglas (1996) *A Pub on Every Corner* Hallamshire Press, Sheffield

Trade Directories, CEBs and Licensing Magistrates Records in Sheffield Local Studies Library and Archives.

Lamb Douglas (2000) *Last Orders* Pickard Publishing, Sheffield

Liversidge Michael (1999) *A definitive A-Z guide of Sheffield's Public Houses* Pickard Publishing, Sheffield

For Churches

Odom Rev W (1917) *Fifty Years of Sheffield Church Life*. JW Northend. Sheffield

Booker AW (1939) *A History of Heeley Wesley Chapel* Private Publication

Childhood and Schools

Mercer Malcolm (1996) *Schooling the Poorer Child* Sheffield Academic Press

Life

Walton Mary (1968) *Sheffield: its story and its achievements*

Leisure

Farnsworth K. (1995) *Sheffield Football* The Hallamshire Press. (Volume 1+2)

Hillerby B.D. (1996) *The Lost Theatres of Sheffield* Wharncliffe Publishing

Transport

Lewis Brian, Clayton Ian (eds) (1994) *Sheffield on Wheels* Yorkshire Art Circus

Vickers J.E. (1972) *From horses to Atlanteans: the story of Sheffield's transport through the ages*

Heeley History Workshop

The Heeley History Workshop was started as a class of the Sheaf Valley Adult Education Sector with its headquarters at Mount Pleasant, Sharrow nearly twenty years ago.

Heeley Bank Community Rooms, in the old Heeley Bank School, have been the venue for regular meetings of the group ever since. With the formation of colleges of further education in Sheffield, the Heeley History Workshop came under first Granville and then Norton colleges. For the last ten years the group has been independent of any college connection.

For the first Sheffield Local History Fair, held in the Town Hall, the Heeley History Workshop produced a short booklet in March 1986 on some aspects of history in Heeley. This was so successful that it was decided to produce a second and so on. Over thirty of these booklets have now been produced plus specials on Sport, Heeley at War and Meersbrook Park. Some back issues and photocopies of these booklets are still available.

The Heeley History Workshop has continued to take a stand at the Sheffield Local History Fairs and has put on displays at Heeley Church to coincide with Heeley Festival each year.

Contact the Heeley History Workshop via:

Lilian Haywood
64 Northcote Road, Heeley, Sheffield, S2 3AU

Or e-mail: linda@moderate.free-online.co.uk

Or see the website at:
http://www.oldheeley.supanet.com

The Heeley History Workshop meets regularly on Monday afternoons from 1.30pm onwards at the Heeley Bank Community Rooms at the corner of Heeley Bank Road and Myrtle Road except Bank Holidays.

There is no formal membership system, no annual subscription and no obligation to attend every week. Visitors are welcome, new regular members are very welcome. Some people only drop in when they can, others attend nearly every session. Some members call in when they are in the area for a visit if normally they live outside Heeley, Sheffield or even the country! Some members from other parts of the world write or e-mail on a regular basis for or with news or to ask for help in Sheffield based research.

Visitors to the display in Heeley Church during Heeley Festival 2000

Topics range from the results of archive research by members, news from letters received by members of relatives or friends previously living in Heeley to general discussions covering many aspects of family and social history in Heeley. Members reminisce about aspects of life in Heeley similar to the topics included in this book or discuss articles or letters brought in by other members.

Over the years we have acquired a large number of photographs both old and more recent of Heeley. These can be copied and originals returned to their owners if they wish. We would be happy to receive any photographs, letters, books or any other memorabilia of the Heeley district. Even if you don't know all the people on a photo bring it along, our members can often help identify them for you. The smallest items of trivia might be interesting to someone else, receipts, posters, programmes of events, leaflets, advertisements, bus tickets even! The list is endless, but we can assure you of a good home for your articles. Our photograph collection is presently being stored on CD-ROM as a supplementary project to the publication of this book and all additions will be welcomed.

Lilian Haywood

Chairperson of the Heeley History Workshop. A career in education started as a teacher in a Grammar School then she moved to Further and then Higher Education, lecturing in Biological and Environmental Sciences, Human Anatomy, Physical and Health Education. She has been a chief examiner in O and A levels and Nursing exams. An active member of NASO for years she is currently its National President. Lilian has written much of the linking material in the Rural to Industrial, Childhood and Life chapters of this book.

Eddie Chapman

Perhaps the oldest resident of Heeley. Now 98 years 'young' and due for his 99th birthday in January 2001, he has lived in the parish all his life. He is an authority on Heeley, which is dear to his heart. Working in the cutlery trade for nearly 60 years, he retired as a 'little mester' at the age of 72. He still regularly attends the Church of the Nazarene and is a much loved and respected member of the community.

Linda Hutton

A relatively new member of the Heeley History Workshop, Linda only came along to do some research for her Open University projects! Two years later, after the completion of her History degree, she has been accepted to study for an MPhil on aspects of Heeley's development in the 19th century. Linda is also a member of the Campaign for Real Ale and did the research on Pubs in Heeley for this book.

Sid Wetherill

Sid was born in Nether Edge in 1927 and moved to Heeley in 1936. His family was the first to move onto the new Northcote Estate. Still living in Heeley now, Sid married a local girl. His interests include collecting old photographs and other information and memorabilia about Heeley.

Betty Renshaw

A retired Assistant Headteacher and History graduate, Betty no longer lives in Heeley, but having been a resident for forty years, has a great affection for the area and still takes and active interest in its history. She still attends Heeley Parish Church where she has been an active member for many years and the organist for more than a decade. Betty has carried out much research into the Church in Heeley and especially Canon Odom.

Joan Palfreyman

Joan is the Treasurer of the Heeley History Workshop and is a long standing member. She was born in Denmark Road, Heeley and has lived in only two homes both of them in the area.

Joyce Jenkinson

Joyce was born in South View Crescent, Highfield to parents Stanley and Louie Boot. She has a brother Eric and sister Doreen both younger than herself. Her father was born in Alexandra Road, Heeley and was christened at Heeley Parish Church. When at Sharrow Lane school she developed a love of history, her other interests include music and reading.

David Smith

David is 59 years old and was born in Heeley and has lived in Heeley all his life. He is interested in the general history of Sheffield and its industrial trades. He has been a member of the Heeley History Workshop for the past four years. He is also a keen photographer.

Ken Burton

Ken moved to Heeley when he got married. He has ancestors buried in Heeley Churchyard who lived in the Newfield Green area. Ken carries out research into Heeley in the Sheffield Archives and Local Studies Library.

Alun Montgomery

Alun is a retired teacher and languages graduate. He was brought up in Heeley where he lived for nearly forty years. 'Naturally I still have an affection for the area and am interested in its history'.

Ray Renshaw

A retired teacher, Ray is from Ridgeway, Derbyshire. He is a member of the Heeley History Workshop by 'adoption'! Husband of Betty, he is also an active member of Heeley Parish Church and spends many hours in the area.
Ray was responsible for the artwork facing page 1.

Photograph and Illustration Acknowledgments

Sheffield Local Library   Inside front cover, pages 3, 3, 5, 9, 11, 13, 15, 17, 18, 18, 20, 21, 21, 22, 26, 26, 28, 28, 30, 31, 33, 34, 36, 36, 38, 51, 52, 54, 58, 59, 60, 65, 66, 69, 75, 76, 79, 80, 82, Inside back cover.

Sheffield Local Studies - permission from Mrs Firth   page 23

Sheffield Archives   page 25

Sheffield Star   page 66

Alun Montgomery   page 88
Aubrey Langhorn   page 68
Betty Renshaw   page 87
David Smith   pages 1, 19, 27, 34, 65, 73, 84, 86, 87, 88
David Staves   page 87
Eddie Chapman   pages 6, 16, 43
Evelyn Wright   page 57
Frances Mary Wilkinson   page 32
Fred Skelton   pages 32, 64
Heeley History Workshop   pages 10, 17, 35, 37
James Birkett   page 25
Joan Palfreyman   page 88
Joyce Jenkinson   pages 14, 88
Ken Burton   page 88
Lilian Haywood   pages 12, 47, 87
Linda Hutton   pages 8, 11, 14, 15, 20, 23, 24, 27, 29, 40, 67, 70, 76, 96
Mary Barker   pages 45, 46, 57
Mavis Thornhill   pages 44, 50, 58
Mrs A Bell   page 1
Mrs Bussey   pages 62, 63
Mrs Doris Pilecki   page 81
Mrs Marsden   page 22
Ray Renshaw   page 88
Sid Wetherill   pages 6, 9, 41, 54, 87
Sylvia Wright   page 56
Winifred M Fanshawe   page 50

Index

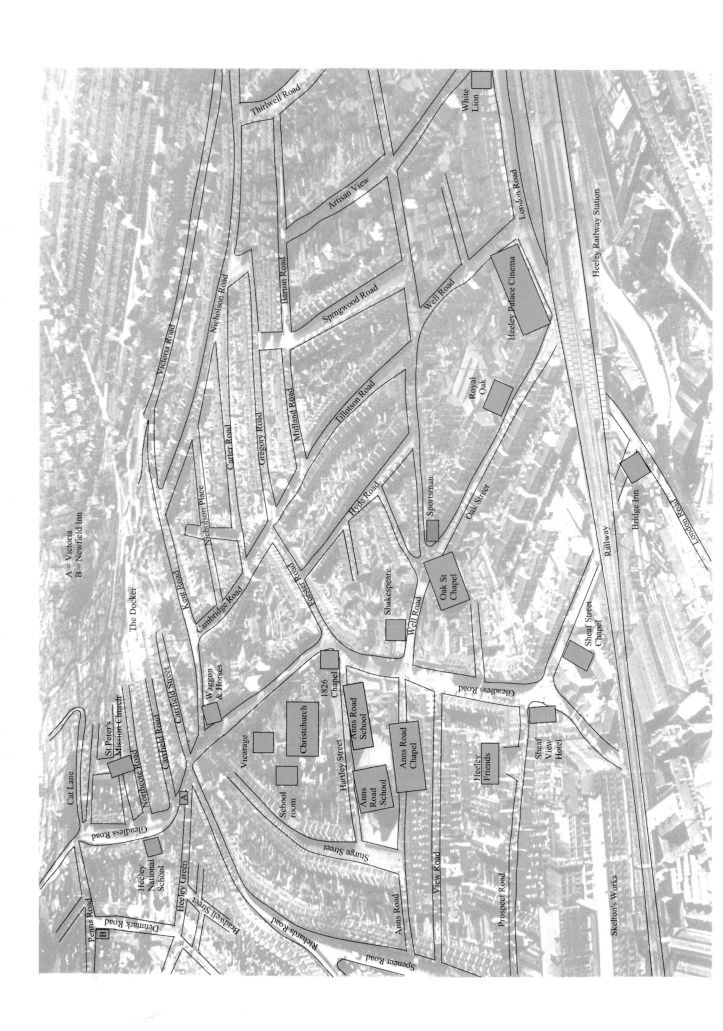

A = Victoria
B = Newfield Inn

Thirlwell Road

Artisan View

White Lion

Springwood Road

Barton Road

London Road

Heeley Railway Station

Nicholson Road

Heeley Palace Cinema

Victoria Road

Well Road

Carter Road

Gregory Road

Midland Road

Tillotson Road

Royal Oak

Oak Street

Nicholson Place

Hyde Road

Sportsman

Kent Road

Foster Road

Shakespeare

Well Road

Oak St Chapel

Railway

Bridge Inn

London Road

Cambridge Road

The Docker

Gleadless Road

Sheaf Street Chapel

Carfield Street

Waggon & Horses

1826 Chapel

Anns Road School

Sheaf View Hotel

St Peter's Mission Church

Carfield Road

Vicarage

Christchurch

Hartley Street

Anns Road Chapel

Heeley Friends

Cat Lane

Northcote Road

School room

Anns Road School

Gleadless Road

Heeley National School

Heeley Green

Sturge Street

View Road

Prospect Road

Penns Road

Denmark Road

Bradwell Street

Richards Road

Anns Road

Spencer Road

Skelton's Works